Chris Schimel's life and character inspire many; and for good reason. He understands and is able to relay the practical encouragement that assists others in their own private journeys.

—JACK W. HAYFORD, PRESIDENT
INTERNATIONAL FOURSQUARE CHURCHES
KINGS INSTITUTE AND KINGS SEMINARY

Touch One is an insightful read that has changed my whole perspective on church growth and ministering to the lost. It's not about the masses; it's about the individual.

—PAM PORTER, PROJECT MANAGER
LONGMONT, COLORADO

Thanks, Chris, for sharing your journey with me. I found myself traveling with you as you unearthed a wealth of insight and understanding concerning what real ministry is about. This is truly a book to heal other travelers!

—JIM STAMP, PASTOR
PARKER COMMUNITY FOURSQUARE CHURCH
PARKER, COLORADO

This honest, soul-searching story is for anyone who cares about people and desires to make a difference. It brings encouragement and direction for those who are "weary in well-doing" and portrays the simplicity of loving as Christ loves. This book is a breath of fresh air that brings life and hope to the wounded, weary clergy, who I often encounter.

—TERRY L. PARKS, MARRIAGE AND
FAMILY THERAPIST
BAKERSFIELD, CALIFORNIA

The desire to be more effective and faithful often prompts us to drive others and ourselves in unhealthy, competitive ways. Chris Schimel candidly confesses this cancer of competitiveness in his own heart and prompts me to once again admit its presence in my own.

—ALAN ALGRIM, SR. PASTOR
ROCKY MOUNTAIN CHRISTIAN CHURCH
NIWOT, COLORADO

Fantastic read! Once I started, I couldn't stop reading. *Touch One* is true to the everyday life of a pastor. Pastor Schimel's stories and examples help us to look at our motives for being in ministry. A must-read for every pastor, future pastor, and ministry leader.

—BOBBY MURRIETA, PASTOR
TRIUMPHANT LIFE CHURCH
WORCESTER, MASSACHUSETTS

When I consider reading a book, my first concern has to do with the character of the author; it will generally be reflected in his or her work. That is why I was anxious to read Chris Schimel's book. I have known him as a person of commitment and integrity for about thirty-five years and in various relationships; first as student–teacher in a college environment, then in a senior pastor–youth pastor relationship, and for several years as fellow pastors. Through all these years, Chris has striven his best to succeed. His book deals with the pain and joy of that journey. Christian leaders can avoid the stress Chris worked through by learning how he discovered what success is…and isn't.

—HAROLD E. HELMS, RETIRED PASTOR,
TEACHER, CHURCH LEADER, AUTHOR
BAKERSFIELD, CALIFORNIA

TOUCH ONE

CHRIS SCHIMEL

CREATION HOUSE
A STRANG COMPANY

Touch One by Chris Schimel
Published by Creation House
A Strang Company
600 Rinehart Road
Lake Mary, Florida 32746
www.creationhouse.com

Unless otherwise noted, all Scripture quotations are from the New King James Version of the Bible. Copyright © 1979, 1980, 1982 by Thomas Nelson, Inc., publishers. Used by permission.

Based on a true story: some names, locations, and times have been changed to protect privacy, and some fiction is included for dramatic purposes. The events of this book occurred over a two-and-a-half-year period in the city of Northridge, California, from 1991 to 1994.

Cover design by Terry Clifton

Library of Congress Control Number: 2007920198
International Standard Book Number: 978-1-59979-181-4

First Edition

07 08 09 10 11 — 9 8 7 6 5 4 3 2 1
Printed in the United States of America

In Loving Dedication...

This book is dedicated to the many friends and family members who have supported Shirley and me and have helped to make possible the publishing of this work.

Joseph and Catherine LaPorte, Tom LaPorte, Sam LaPorte, Chuck and Terry Parks, Pam Porter, Ann Porter, Joe and Esther Campanella, Kevin and Sharon Cox, Bob and Betty Campanella, Sal and Dorothy Pecoraro, Bonnie Krall, Tony and Frances Gligora, Robert Pitto, and Lauren Humdy.

And, a very special thanks to life-long friends and partners in ministry: Andrew and Dayle Lum and Jerry and Korena Rothlisberger who have demonstrated undying support and belief in our ministry.

CONTENTS

See the Beauty

For years now God has allowed me to catch glimpses of the *beauty* of His bride, the church. Many are very skilled at noticing the ugly and tainted aspects of His family on Earth. Actually, if the truth were known, I am quite adept at spotting the church's grotesque leanings as well. It is a skill my carnal nature has developed quite nicely over the span of my life. Lately, however, it has been the *beauty* of His body that has been getting my attention.

In *Touch One* you will not only see some ugliness-spotting skills, you will also see that my heart, all by itself, models some of those ugly qualities. But if you keep reading, you will see a beautiful aspect of His church unfold, and hopefully you will see my heart change from something painful to look at into something more beautiful and pleasing before God.

As you read this astounding story that God brought my way, may I suggest that you try to adjust your perception sensors so that you too can see the *beauty* of God's bride amid its imperfections.

You've been to weddings. You've seen the brides. Some are short and some are tall. Some are thin and some more robust. Some are stressed and stern while others are relaxed and joyful. But what stands out is how beautiful she looks in her spotless white dress, her hairdo shaped to precision, the glow on her face, and the unmistakable air of elegance she carries on her red-letter day. Some may broach thoughts that there are flaws in some aspect of her appearance or attitude, but most know that to allow those thoughts to wander into full-blown opinions is not allowed—not on the most important day of her life. All we are allowed to see is her *beauty*. You've seen her *beauty*, haven't you?

As you read this incredible account, *see the beauty* of God's church, His bride. *See the beauty* of hearts in His kingdom that genuinely care about people. *See the beauty* of how important one life is to God—and how important He wants that one life to be to you and me.

PREFACE

For one brief moment I was a hero.

I was born and raised in a small town in New York state. High school sports always were, and continue to be, my hometown's primary reason for existence. The high school basketball team had not played for the championship for twelve years and we were getting very hungry for the opportunity again.

Our team qualified to play in the semi-final match, the winner of which would make the trip down the highway to Buffalo the next week to play in the section six championship. That game was played in the Buffalo Memorial Auditorium, the soon-to-be home of the professional basketball team, the Buffalo Braves.

Our archrivals also maneuvered their way into the semifinal game. We had not beaten them in the last few years in anything, so our senses were filled with both fear and resolve.

The game found us one point behind with less than a minute to play. With thirty seconds left in the game, in heroic fashion, I made a basket and a foul shot to put us over the top and send us victoriously into the championship game.

When the final buzzer sounded, the entire population of our town, all of which it seemed were in attendance, rushed the floor and surrounded the team with cheers and adulation. Three or four players hoisted me onto their shoulders and carried me off the floor. The euphoria of that moment has gone almost unparalleled throughout most of my life.

That was the *glory* of the event. The *reality* of the event looked much different.

The truth is, our coach played the same five players the entire game, because he felt they were the only ones on the team he could count on. With *thirty-eight seconds* left in the contest, and our team one point down, our starting point guard—the team star—sprained his ankle and could not continue.

I was one of three point guards on the team. None of us offered a great deal of strength that year off the bench. You could see the dilemma the coach was in at that crucial moment.

For a few brief seconds he paced back and forth in front of the bench. We all watched him with bated breath waiting to spring into action should he call one of our names. Personally, from hindsight, what I saw on his countenance was anguish. I can still see nearly forty years later the battle that was being fought within him. He was afraid of what any one of us might do to our team's chances for a victory. I couldn't see it then; I could only see the possible opportunity before me.

Finally, with great apprehension, he looked at me and

said, "Schimel, go in for Larsen."

I sprang from the bench and headed for the statistician's table to report in.

To intensify the drama my coach grabbed me by the arm as I crossed in front of him and pleaded with me, "Please, don't screw up!"

It didn't shake me, though—at least, not any more than I was already shaken. I had my own inner issues to deal with. As much as I was excited to play, I didn't enter the game with a confident and determined attitude. I entered the game in a fog.

The crowd packed the gymnasium we played in so tightly there wasn't room enough in it to *change your mind*, much less your position. Every voice in the place was screaming at the peak of its capabilities. The sound was deafening.

The clock started and play began, but it didn't feel to me that I was even there. It felt as if I were off in some misty, overgrown forest miles away from everyone.

When I received a pass on the left wing, my man happened to be out of position, so I broke for the hoop. It almost felt, however, that I was in some other dimension of time. When I laid the ball up toward the basket, my head felt hollow. The sound in the building was so overwhelming, if you can imagine, it made me feel as if I were the only one in the place. No one blocked the shot. No one even touched me on my way to the basket. The shot slipped up over the rim and through the net without even a hint of opposition, almost as though, in that moment, time froze, and with it every player on the floor except me.

I didn't think the crowd could rise to a higher pitch than

it was before the basket, but the sudden blast of cheers that followed corrected my errant assumption. Strangely, however, that made me feel even more as if I were on the court in complete solitude. There were other players running around wearing different colored jerseys, but in my mind, I was alone.

Later, with seventeen seconds left, I was fouled and made one of the free throws I threw toward the basket, putting us two points ahead.

"They were the only three points he scored in the game," the radio announcer said in the game summary. "But they were the most important three points of the contest."

The next week during practice, in preparation for the championship, it seemed my shot was all the coach could talk about. He demonstrated it several times before the team and, toward the end of the week, announced that I would be in the starting lineup for the championship game. I am sure he thought by accident he discovered something about me he hadn't seen before—that I was able to come through in the clutch. And what game could be more a clutch situation than the championship?

He found out very quickly that his judgments about me were quite incorrect. I guess I had too much time to think about that game, because I began to flub up from the opening tip off and was benched early. The fact that I played for only *thirty-eight seconds* in the semi-final game, the pain on my coaches face, the fog I played in, and the poor showing I displayed in the next game all combined to demonstrate the reality of that event.

It was *thirty-eight seconds of glory*—that's all. Yet I have seemed to live much of my life in the *glory* of that event, rather than the *reality* of it.

I tend to be very idealistic. I see the best, think the best, and live in denial concerning the worst in most every scenario in my life—and I like the *glory*. But the *glory* for most of us is not *reality*. Reality includes failure. It includes struggling, pain, hurt, and learning to go on in spite of the anguish.

In my life I saw success as *glory*. The acclaim, recognition, and *glory* that leaders of large churches received all seemed like the success those fateful *thirty-eight seconds* presented to me in the spring of 1968. That is what I have always wanted, and it seems I have spent much of my ministry seeking after that same euphoria over and over again. Anything less felt like failure to me.

One very average day I walked through the sanctuary of the church I led in Northridge, California, and prayed a very simple prayer with heartfelt passion and sincerity.

Lord, help me to really make a difference.

I'm sure I thought if God answered that prayer, the answer would come to me packaged in a way that would look like those momentous *thirty-eight seconds*, with a few variations perhaps. I didn't know how absolutely unlike those *thirty-eight seconds* God's answer to my prayer would be.

CHAPTER 1

Over the Edge

My office faced the front parking lot of our church and overlooked the boulevard on which our building was located. I didn't have a secretary to intercept the issues that came to our front door, because our church did not have enough income to afford one. So my office, being in the front, was *good news* and *bad news*. When deliveries, appointments, or visitors interested in our church came by, I was right there to catch them before they would wander through the complex and get lost. That was *good*. But when undesirables dropped in, such as belligerent beggars, obnoxious salespeople, or disgruntled critics of Christianity, there was no escape. Believe me, that was *bad* news.

I have had sellers of goods keep me for hours, trying to sell me something I would never use in a hundred lifetimes.

Once a very large, mean-looking homeless person came in begging for cash. I suspected trouble the minute I saw him. There was no money on the property, and I was flat broke. When I refused him he cussed me out, picked a book up off my desk, threw it across the room, and slammed my door, breaking it on the way out. He then sat down on the front lawn of the church and stared at me through my office window. I had to call the police and have him removed before I could leave to go home.

Another time a critic of Christianity came to my door. Actually that title doesn't do him justice. It would be more accurate to say he was a hater of all Christian principles from Christianity's inception to the present day. And he was fired up about it. He was moderately hostile for the entire ninety minutes he kept me, and I couldn't get away from him. Some drop-ins can be extremely scary.

You can understand my concern when I saw a strange gentleman peer through my window, cupping his hands around his eyes to shield the glare.

When he saw that I was there, he came to my door and knocked. I took a deep breath, rose from my chair, and walked over to my office door.

Opening it, I said to the man, "May I help you?"

"Can I talk to you?" he asked rather abruptly.

"About what?" I responded.

I knew I was in trouble when he said in a harsh tone, "Can I talk to you or not?"

I was taken aback, yet something kept me from refusing him.

I said in a submitted manner, "Sure. Fine. Come on in. Have a seat."

He sat down and stared straight ahead.

I asked, "What is your name?"

He shot back at me, "No names, do you understand? I don't have a name, and you don't have a name. If you have a problem with that, then we can end this right now."

What he didn't know was that I would have been very willing to end it right then. I was already contemplating how I would escape, should he freak out and attempt to come after me.

But I sheepishly responded, "No, that's fine. No names is fine."

The next two hours were two of the most frightening, and yet weird, hours of my life. He shouted. He screamed. He paced. He pounded on the wall. He crawled on the floor. He kicked. He hated. He shook. He jumped up and down.

At times I felt like crying. Other times I was choking back the laughter. Most of the time I didn't know what to say, so I just listened. When the silence became too uncomfortable I tried to speak what I thought might be appropriate words, only to be screamed at and told to shut up.

The words he shouted, screamed, cried, and squeezed out of his throat all had to do with the corruption in our world and on the streets.

"I hate people. I hate this world. I hate God, and I hate myself," were the clear words I heard him speak many times during those two hours. But mostly he just made sounds that revealed an anguished and troubled heart. I certainly felt very sorry for the man, but I thought I was in the presence of a raving lunatic, and I couldn't wait for him to leave.

Finally he sat down and became quiet for several minutes. Then he looked at me and said calmly, "No one is to know I was here. Do you promise you won't tell anyone?"

I said, "I won't tell anyone. You have my word."

And with that he was gone. He walked out the door and disappeared.

For the longest time I sat and stared straight ahead, reflecting on what just happened. I was emotionally drained and didn't feel capable of jumping back into working on my sermon, so I just sat there and pondered. As I thought about the previous two hours, I smiled, wept, and sat in awe of the man who just invaded my life.

I tried to imagine what could have set him off the way it did. Was he a murderer or some other type of criminal? Was he an asylum escapee or a post office employee? It would certainly make sense, considering what I just experienced with him. Honestly, I was clueless. I certainly had no idea what put him over the edge, and I had no idea this man would change my life.

When I collected myself I knelt down beside my chair and prayed for this very mixed up person. I tried to work after that, but the incident completely broke my concentration, so I fiddled for a while, packed up my briefcase, locked the office, and left for the day.

That night I found myself wanting to tell my wife, Shirley, about the bizarre incident that happened to me that day, but in the end I decided to honor the anonymity the man requested from me.

CHAPTER 2

Serving

Iforgot all about the man who came into my office that day. I lost remembrance of him in a sea of serving.

Soon after that several very difficult crises emerged within the group of people that made up our church. It was most peculiar for a church our size to have so many painful issues going on all at once, and because of my heartfelt desire to see ever-increasing numbers of people pour into my church, helping just *one* person at a time seemed wearisome to me. It seemed like slow going toward my growth goals. I still had that *thirty-eight seconds of glory* (mentioned in the preface) well in focus. Although I was having trouble getting into caring for individuals, it seemed as if God, or some unseen force, were trying to plunge me, against my will, into a ministry pattern that would demand my focus on the needs of people under my care. For the next few months it seemed all I had time for were individuals. I didn't have time to plan, dream, or strategize about how I was going to get our church to grow. Reading books or listening to tapes on the subject was out of the question. There wasn't time to meet with leadership for strategy sessions. Getting bigger was the furthest thing from my mind, because my mind was over-occupied with the needs of people.

One incident involved a lady who began attending our church. Her name was Penny. Before coming to our church Penny and her family had not been going to any church for some time. Their previous church became uncomfortable. They felt judged and rejected because of some issues that arose in her family.

Penny married a man of another race, and all her children bore the physical signs. Initially this wasn't a problem, but over time, when other issues arose, this fact seemed to become part of the problem. It was understood by more people than just Penny that her husband had a growing list of ladies he was seeing on the side. This was painful enough for Penny, but then she began to receive raised eyebrows and judgmental, blame-ridden advice from people she expected would support her. Much of the advice carried with it racial suggestions such as, "Didn't you know men of that race typically have problems like this." The real difficulty was that her kids would always reflect their racial mix, and in time they would be judged also.

In addition Penny's adult son, who was in his early twenties, contracted AIDS through a homosexual encounter. This further increased the awkwardness and judgment she felt from people in her church.

To heighten the tension Penny's nineteen-year-old daughter began getting into trouble. When they came to our church Penny's daughter was awaiting a court trial for writing fraudulent checks. If that weren't enough Penny had another teenage daughter, Miranda, with a different set of issues. Miranda possessed a physical deformity—a very obvious hunched back. She began experiencing some alienation from kids her age perhaps because of the deformity, perhaps as fallout from the other family issues, perhaps from all of it.

It all caused Penny to feel hurt, confused, and needing to protect her family from the stares and pointed fingers they were starting to receive. Sadly, she left the church she attended for many years, because she felt it would be damaging to her family to stay.

Enough time went by, and she now felt up to the challenge. She made a positive connection with one of our members, so she thought she would give our church a try. She and Miranda, her only child living at home, came to our church expecting the same resistance but hoping it wouldn't be so. Our people felt only compassion for them.

Through all of this Penny sought comfort and support. I found that I was fairly consumed with the trauma she and Miranda experienced. Penny's situation, however, was not the only crisis that settled upon our church around that time.

Another family had a two-year-old son named Jacob. After what they thought was a minor fall, Jacob was suddenly in great pain and unable to walk. His parents took him to the emergency room where they discovered his leg was broken in three places. The doctors informed them that Jacob would need to be in a three-quarter body cast for up to six months. To complicate matters even more, civil service was brought into the situation, because the incident looked a lot like child abuse. His parents spent several weeks trying to convince the powers that be that they were not abusive parents. When they finally cleared themselves of these suspicions with the state of California, they were still left with an absolutely dependent, frustrated, and confused two-year-old.

I wish that were all that was going on in our church at that time, but alas, it was not.

Pete was hopelessly addicted to cocaine for more than ten years. He voluntarily entered programs for his problem. These programs were such that they isolated Pete in remote settings for six months to a year, while attempting to beat his problem. I visited him on more than one occasion in the desert hills of southern California at the institution where he stayed. During my last visit he requested something. He asked if I would approach his parents about his coming home to visit them over a weekend.

Pete was in this program for four months and qualified for a weekend pass. Pete's mom regularly attended our church, and his dad attended periodically. They ejected Pete from their house several years before because of his drug addiction and related problems, and they were adamant about his staying away until he rid himself of his destructive habit.

When I approached Pete's mother with his request, she was overjoyed. She had not seen or heard a word from her son in more than a year. She persuaded Pete's dad to let him come, so the weekend was set.

Pete arrived home around five o'clock on a Friday night, and the homecoming was a happy one.

Drugs plagued Pete for more than a decade. When he was heavy into his habit, all morality seemed to elude him, including respect for his parents. He had no conscience about stealing from them to pay for drugs when necessary. Before entering the program, Pete gave his black Ford Ranger to his parents. He did this partly to make up for the havoc he caused them and the many times he stole from them, but also partly because he couldn't make the payments while he was in the drug program.

At seven o'clock on the day he arrived home, he asked his parents for the truck to run to a store to grab a soda. They let him go, and it was the beginning of one of the most horrific weekends in all of our lives.

Pete had no intention of buying a soda. He wasn't thirsty for Coke; he was thirsty for cocaine. He found an old connection and, since he had no money, traded the use of his parents' truck for a bag of the white power. He made short order of that bag and quickly collected himself enough to find his way to the rendezvous point in time to get the truck back. To the surprise of everyone who knows how these kinds of drug deals work, the people who traded drugs for the use of the truck were actually there with the vehicle. But instead of taking the truck back and going home, Pete traded use of the vehicle a second time for more drugs.

What do these drug dealers do with automobiles they trade their drugs for? They use them for more than joy rides. They use the vehicles themselves or rent them to someone else for use in crimes. It is much safer than stealing a car, because stolen cars get recorded into the police database, and the drivers, if caught, can easily go down for the crime. A car traded for drugs, however, is not reported as stolen. That gives the criminals more opportunity to ditch the vehicle and put time and distance between themselves and the crime they committed. It also raises questions about the possibility that the true perpetrator of the crime was the owner of the vehicle, especially if the owner is a drug user like Pete.

After Pete wasted himself on the second bag of cocaine, it was five o'clock on Saturday, a full twenty-four hours after he arrived home from rehab on the weekend pass. He was supposed to connect with the people he dealt with at six o'clock, but this time they didn't show. Pete began to comb the streets on foot, his eyes searching frantically for his truck. He got lucky and spotted the truck cruising down the street he was on. There were two people inside, and they passed him, not knowing he was the owner. Pete immediately threw his skinny but hyped up body into a dead run. As luck would have it, the truck became stuck between cars at a red light.

Pete ran at his Ford Ranger, screaming, "That's my truck! That's my truck!"

The two men inside weren't the ones Pete originally dealt with, so they didn't recognize him. Their initial reaction was panic, and they both abandoned Pete's truck at the red light and ran off down a side street.

This is where the story gets bizarre, but it speaks of the power of cocaine.

Pete jumped into the driver's seat of his miraculously recaptured vehicle and breathed a sigh of relief as he drove it away when the light turned green. Less than a block from that light, Pete turned the vehicle around again and headed for his usual connection, to yet a third time, and after two close calls, trade his truck for another bag of the devil's blend.

It was then late on Saturday night. He did his drugs and when the truck didn't show up at the next rendezvous point, he spent the night on the street.

Meanwhile I received several calls from Pete's mother beginning late Friday night. We were praying for Pete's safety and for the preserved sanity of his mom and dad. None of us had any idea concerning Pete's whereabouts. And yet, we all had a suspicion about what was really going on.

On Sunday afternoon at four o'clock there was a knock at my door. When I opened it, there was Pete. He was dressed only in a pair of black cut-offs. He was covered with sweat from his head to his feet, and his short brown hair was completely disheveled.

His first words were, "I need help."

I invited him in. He sat down and told me the entire story of that weekend.

When he finished he said, "I need a ride to meet my AA sponsor. Can I use your phone?"

He dialed a number, took the cordless receiver with him into the hallway of our home, mumbled a few words over the phone, and returned.

"Can you give me a ride now?" he asked sheepishly.

Shirley and I were scheduled to be at a dinner meeting, and we were about to go out the door. I told Pete that we could only give him a ride to his sponsor's house because of time. I gave him some clothes to wear, and after he put them on we piled into my car.

I followed Pete's directions as he guided us onto the local freeway, off an exit, and down a side street toward his sponsor's house.

Suddenly Pete screamed, "Turn around! Turn around right now."

"Why?" I asked in a panicked tone, scared by the volume of his voice.

"Just turn around," he said. "I saw something."

I made a quick u-turn when the coast was clear and started driving down the street in the opposite direction.

"Now, what did you see?" I demanded.

"My truck. Just keep going. I see it. It's just a few lights ahead. Do you have anything I can use for a weapon—a tire iron or a wrench or something?"

I screeched to a halt beside the curb and screamed at him, "No way, Pete. My wife is here in the car with us. They could have guns. I am not going to jeopardize my life, my wife's life, and even yours for your stupid truck."

Pete screamed back at me, "But I have to get it back!" We argued back and forth for a few minutes until he finally conceded.

I waited until I calmed myself down. Then I pulled slowly away from the curb and made the necessary turns to head us back in the direction of his sponsor's house.

We pulled up front. Pete nervously scurried out of the car and insincerely thanked us for the ride. He walked toward the front door and disappeared into the house.

Pete's mother came back to our church one time, sat in the back, and left the service early. I tried to phone her, but she never returned my calls. Later I learned that Pete's truck was found on some blocks and stripped of everything valuable. I also learned through the grapevine that Pete's mom didn't really blame me for the horrid weekend, but had trouble separating me from it.

These three major scenarios happened at the same time

and were certainly enough to occupy the pastor of a small church. However, there was more going on in our fellowship around that time.

Fred and Terry were getting a divorce. She was nowhere to be found. She ran off with a guy she met and wasn't heard from again until the divorce was final.

Tom and his family were trying to start a new life after he served a year's sentence in prison for embezzlement. They came to our church confused and needing a lot of love and attention.

Sharon was distraught, because she and her husband were unable to have a child.

Patty had been abused by her father for several years while growing up, and the time came when she would need to deal seriously with her issues and confront her dad.

Paula found out that her father had been engaging in inappropriate sexual behavior with her daughter—his own granddaughter—while babysitting her. The whole family attended our church.

There was still more. It was an avalanche of difficult situations that seemed to come at me all at once.

If I had had time to analyze these incidents in package form, I might have stopped up short and queried, "Wait a minute. What is going on here, anyway?" But I didn't. I just put my blinders on, thereby eliminating the bulk of the distractions, and got through it. Our church seemed to weather this time as well.

During this time I was asked to speak at a chapel service for a Bible college in my area. As I prepared I was impressed that God wanted me to tell the students about how I was spending my time lately.

I remembered back to when I sat in the seats they were sitting in and held unrealistic expectations concerning what the ministry was supposed to be. With that, I felt my task that day was to help these students gain a more realistic perspective on ministry than I had so many years before.

I began, "I'd like to introduce you to some people in our church. First, I would like you to meet Penny. Penny has a daughter awaiting trial for check fraud, a son with AIDS, and another daughter with a severe physical deformity. She is desperate for love and acceptance."

"I would also like to introduce you to Jacob. He is two years old and right now is in a three-quarter body cast and will be for several months. Authorities are questioning his parents because Jacob's injuries look like child abuse to them. I pray with them about their dilemma most days."

"I would also like to introduce you to Pete," and I went on naming and describing each of the scenarios I described in this chapter and several more—twelve in all.

Then I said, "Perhaps you have certain ideas concerning what the ministry is about. But I want you to know, this is the ministry: helping hurting people."

I recall how quiet it was in the chapel service when I finished my introductions. I don't know whether I shocked the audience into reality or just depressed them. Regardless of what they felt, it was clear to me that I was feeling things deeply. I think that was the first time I felt genuine empathy and personal pain for the people under my care. God was definitely working on me.

CHAPTER 3

Client

Would I be able to talk with you?" I heard a voice ask
behind me.

I was doing some work on the platform of the church
auditorium and had my back to the rear entrance. I turned
around when I heard the voice and was surprised to see the
crazy man who filled my office with his fury a few months
before. Upon seeing him I felt instant apprehension.

"Hi," I said tentatively, hoping my discomfort wasn't
obvious. "Uh, sure. Just let me put this away, and I'll be right
there."

I slipped into the side room located off the platform,
bent over, and placed the hammer I had been using into my
toolbox. I stood back up, took a deep breath, and muttered
to myself a few words that expressed my frustration with
being interrupted. Then I went to the back of the church
where the man was waiting for me.

"You weren't in your office, and I saw the door open, so
I thought I'd check to see if you were here," he said deliberately
but apologetically.

"That's fine," I responded. I was sure he must have detected my uneasiness. "Come on in," I said as I gestured for him to follow me into my office.

Upon entering I walked over, stood behind my desk, and motioned for him to sit down. The time before I sat in one of the two guest chairs in front of my desk while he occupied the other. That is usually where I sit when I counsel someone. It is far less formal. After my last encounter with this very unusual individual, however, I figured my desk would serve as a good protective barrier between him and myself just in case one of his psychotic episodes should compel him to go for my throat.

The man didn't sit. He stood in front of the guest chair, placed his hands in the rear pockets of his pants, and just stared straight ahead for what seemed an eternity. I also stood behind my solid oak desk, extremely uneasy, and thinking it was definitely smart of me to place the wooden barricade between us.

The man was of average build and height, perhaps five feet ten inches tall and a thin one hundred seventy-five pounds, but his intensity made him seem much larger. He possessed a worn and drawn countenance. I guessed he was about forty years old, although his facial features made him appear somewhat older. His hair was brown, straight, fine in texture, and slightly thinning. It hung over his forehead and was cut to length about an inch above his eyebrows. He parted his hair from left to right, but I noticed his part was anything but straight. It was apparent that day; he scurried out from wherever he called home without washing his hair, because the hair on one side of his head possessed a slept-on look. It appeared to be matted down, dampened with water, and then combed in an attempt to hide the flattened appearance. The slept-on look, however, stood out quite clearly to me.

Instead of a sports coat and tie, which he wore the first time he showed up at my church, this time he wore a wrinkled, plain-colored shirt and a pair of jeans, which suggested he was paying this visit to me on his day off. That prospect was frightening, because it could mean an all-day counseling session with a complete lunatic. As I pondered that possibility, I swallowed hard.

I made all these observations about him as he stood there motionless. Finally, however, he sat down. When he did I relaxed a bit and lowered myself into my chair as well. I truly felt safer behind my desk.

"You think I'm nuts, don't you?" he asked, turning his head in my direction and looking full into my face.

"No," I lied. "I just think you are going through some pretty intense stuff, that's all."

I knew I wasn't very convincing, but I continued and asked, "What would you like to talk about?"

I never expected that he would show up again. I figured he dumped his truckload of psychosis on me one time and that would be the last I would ever see or hear from him again. Honestly, I was a bit shocked that he was sitting in my office a second time, but it spoke to me that our last meeting was somewhat beneficial to him, no matter what I concluded about the outcome.

At my question he shot out of his chair to a standing position and started to pace as much as anyone could in my rather cramped office.

And I thought, *Here we go.*

"What do I want to talk about? What do I want to talk about?" he repeated loudly as he continued to pace. "Well, I don't want to talk about the human trash that I have to deal with every day. But apparently, that is what I have to talk about, because unless I talk about it, I'm going to go insane."

I thought, *Too late. He's there already.*

By then he was shouting, and as he did, I felt my anxiety level rising to new heights yet to be scaled. Though my body still remained seated I could feel the butterflies in my stomach flying frantically from wall to wall within me. At that moment I knew I was in for another psychotic event at the hands of this mysterious drop-in client. Right then I was really patting myself on the back for having the presence of mind to sit behind my desk.

I didn't say a word for the next half hour. I would like to say it was because I was wisely listening. More truthfully, however, I think it was because I was scared beyond words.

Yet as I listened I learned a few things about this troubled soul. At one point the word *precinct* dropped from his mouth. At another point he referred to the other *detectives* he had to deal with. Still further on in his angry monologue, in trying to skirt around his true profession, he slipped and referred to his *captain,* at which time he stopped abruptly and retorted, "I've said too much. You know what my job is, don't you?"

I was almost afraid to speak. But after a long pause, I said, "If I admit that I know, is my life in danger?"

I wasn't trying to be funny. I was dead serious. I guess

I watch too many movies. I sat there, holding my breath for what seemed forever, staring in a somewhat terrified manner into his eyes as he gazed back into mine.

Finally, he chuckled and said, "Don't worry. I'm not going to hurt you."

I felt a great load lift off of my mind at that moment, more from his smile than his words concerning my safety. That was the first time I saw anything else from him other than seriousness, a lot of craziness, and a great deal of intense anger. It made me feel that perhaps somewhere, deep within his being, there was a real person.

Apparently he could see the relief on my face and said, "Listen, here's the deal. You've probably guessed that I'm a police detective. I can't tell you my name, and I can't tell you what city I work in. If I do you might report me. I know I'm a little nuts right now, but if someone finds out I'm seeing a counselor or a preacher—or whatever you are—they could take my job away. So can I count on you to keep your mouth shut about me?"

"I won't tell a soul," I promised. I was just breathing easier because he ceased shouting, and I actually saw a smile on his face.

Then he took a deep breath, as if he were about to reveal the deepest, darkest secret on Earth and said, "Listen. The psych guys they bring in from time to time are bad news. Last year there was this street cop. I didn't know him, but everyone knows the story. He was acting a little crazy. They brought in a psych guy to talk with him. Within two days, he was off on medical leave and wound up losing his job."

As he told the story his volume grew louder and his

demeanor angrier. His smile was gone, and I could detect both fear and disdain in his voice.

He continued, "Later that year he shot himself through the head. The note he left said, 'I have failed as a police officer, the only job I really loved.'"

At that point he was breathing hard, as if he just sprinted a hundred yards; and he was looking into my eyes as if to plead, "I beg of you, please understand my dilemma."

For a few more seconds he stared into my eyes, pleading and breathing hard. Then he sprang from his seat, whirled around, and stood before my window. Looking out into the smoggy California air, he said, "I can't let on to anyone that anything is wrong. I can't even tell my wife, because if I do, she will squeal to my captain and that will be the beginning of the end."

Then he turned around and walked over to my desk. Leaning on it and facing me, he said, "Now do you understand why I'm here and why there's only so much I can tell you?"

Then he added emphatically, while tapping the knuckles of his closed right fist on my desk, "No psych guy is going to end my career. I have a wife and kids to support, and frankly, I don't know how to do anything else. As much as I hate my job right now, it's all I know."

He didn't say it, but I knew he wanted a once-and-for-all commitment that I would keep our meetings completely confidential. I had no problem with that, but right then I was struck with the weight of the responsibility I was going to have to carry in order to protect his secret.

Before I felt at liberty to give him my answer, he pulled his chair back, sat in it, and said, "It's probably going to be better if you know a little more about me, anyway. That way I can spill my guts about the —— I go through on the streets and not hold anything back. Is it OK if I cuss? That's the way I talk, anyway. I mean, you won't preach at me if I swear, will you?"

"Sure. You can say whatever you feel like saying," I said. But I was just relieved he was talking in whole sentences instead of grunting, groaning, and screaming out incoherent sounds as he had in our first meeting. An occasional cuss word now and then would have suggested that he still had at least somewhat of a grip on reality.

He went on talking, cussing, and shouting for at least another hour. Now and then his communication would be phrased in the form of a question, to which I would offer an answer. But mostly he vented.

As he did I listened and wondered, *How did I end up with this bizarre person? Did God have something in mind for me in all of this? If so, what?*

One thing was certain: this man adopted me as his personal therapist. I hadn't the skill or the education to counsel him. I knew protocol demanded that I refer him to someone more skilled. Yet I was certain the mere mention of this would cause him to bolt and perhaps receive no help from anyone. So here I was, dealing with a stressed-out police detective on the verge of a nervous breakdown. At this thought I became certain I would see him again.

When he rose to leave that day, I assured him I would divulge our meetings to no one. Then he left.

As before, after he exited the door I had a hard time just sliding back into my work. I sat there and thought about what just took place. While he was emoting, unknowingly he was also talking about some of the same situations I dealt with, especially the last several weeks. Some of those situations were still going on.

I thought about his job and mine. We both dealt with difficult situations with intention to help. He protected people from physical danger; I protected people from spiritual danger. I concluded that his job was a lot like mine.

That day, as I considered our different professions, it seemed to me there was one difference. When I looked at the scenarios I attended to in my ministry, I saw hope. When this detective looked at the scenarios he encountered every day, he saw no hope. I thought, *If I saw no hope for the people I served, I would go crazy, too.*

I knelt beside my desk and prayed in a more informed way for him than I prayed before.

I prayed, *Lord, help him to work through his troubles. Help him to learn about the hope there is in you. Give me an opportunity to share with him about that hope.*

CHAPTER 4

Back to School

I was never a big fan of school. I graduated from high school, slipping through by the skin of my teeth. It wasn't for a lack of mental ability that my grades were low; it was clearly a lack of desire. I never wanted to be in class, study, or do homework. Cheating was not a practice I totally rejected. I recall several times when it bailed me out of significant jams. I think at times I even thanked God for the whole concept of cheating.

When I became a Christian and went off to Bible college, I'm happy to report, the cheating discontinued and my grades improved considerably. This was true probably because I was finally studying something that captured my interest, but to say at that time that I began to love academics would be a bold-faced lie. I was still in a dead run to finish my degree so I could get on with life and be through with the classroom once and for all. I even chose the degree that would have me out of school in the least amount of time. Once I was "set free" at graduation, I did not want to go back. A master's or doctorate degree held no interest for me. Once I completed my undergraduate responsibilities, you could not have dragged me back into school—not even with brute force.

For many years I rode the success of my ministry past the front doors of the educational institution, refusing to get off and enter. Sometimes the ride was bumpy. At times it was down right brutal. I can recall several falls off my steed. The last fall, sixteen years after I finished my undergraduate degree, found me getting up, brushing myself off, and walking through the doors to inquire about more education. It took me sixteen years of rugged success rides to realize that if I am going to be effective in reaching the generation I am called to serve, I am going to have to acquire more information.

Although, looking back in retrospect, I think my decision to return to school and secure a graduate degree was still a *success issue*. I asked myself the question: how can I make my church bigger and myself a success? How can I achieve that *thirty-eight seconds of glory* again? I tried many other means, all of which turned out to be dead ends. So my next effort at achieving a big church and more success was a graduate degree.

I went for it highly motivated. I think that early drive to be done with school still had me in a choke hold. In much less time than it should have taken, I finished my graduate degree and did so while I was still a full-time pastor.

Don't get me wrong. Though questionable intentions were woven into my motivation to secure a graduate degree, the education I received was extremely valuable, and I have used it to great advantage as I have served God in the ministry. However, it did not make my church bigger, and it did not bring me any closer to that illusive state of feeling that I was a success in the ministry. When I finally completed my master of divinity degree nearly twenty years after finishing my undergraduate studies, I think I was floundering under the same kind of idealism I exited college with.

I remember well the fanciful dreams and aspirations I had when I first graduated from Bible college. I was twenty-two and truly thought I would be responsible for changing the world all on my own. I was certain that when people heard my explanation and presentation of the gospel, wild horses couldn't keep them away. People would flock to my ministry in droves and the numbers would just keep on increasing.

Yet I had a rude awakening just two months into my first assignment after graduating from Bible college.

My first job out of school was a youth ministry position at a small church in Pennsylvania. Upon arriving there, my wife and I gathered the teenagers of the church together and inquired of them concerning their desire for a first youth activity. Fishing was the consensus. We scheduled the event and made preparations.

I went to the local sports store the day before the event was to take place to buy a fishing license. In Pennsylvania, at that time, to purchase a resident's fishing license, a person was required to have resided in that state a minimum of two months. That was no problem. I had three days to spare. The problem was I possessed no proof that I was an official Pennsylvania resident and had been for over two months. I had not applied for my Pennsylvania driver's license yet, nor did I have any other form of identification verifying my official status as a Pennsylvania resident. Consequently, I spent about half an hour trying to convince the lady at the counter that I had indeed been in the state for at least sixty days, all to no avail. She would not budge.

Finally I resorted to the big guns and did so as I recall with an inner sense of confidence that when she heard my next words, the issue would instantly come to a peaceful conclusion and I would walk away with my fishing license.

I said, "Listen, ma'am. I am a minister. I wouldn't lie to you. Here are my credentials," as I flashed the impressive paperwork before her eyes.

To my utter amazement she responded, "That don't mean no beans to me. What I need is a Pennsylvania driver's license."

I was crushed. It was my first real rejection. It may seem odd, but that very day I became alerted to the possibility that it might be harder to get the masses to respond to me than I originally thought.

My storybook ideas of success early on were akin to the same immaturity I possessed as a person and as a Christian at age twenty-two. Over the years, and one by one, most of my opinions and zealous idealism would be challenged, dismantled, and reconstructed into a framework that would be more pure and pleasing to God and more realistic concerning the world I lived in.

I have struggled with the idea that big is better my whole life. As an athlete in high school and college, any size greater than five feet nine inches and one hundred fifty pounds would have been extremely helpful. I was knocked around in football, outdone in baseball, and in basketball I have never touched the rim in my life. For me the term "white men can't jump" carries profound meaning.

When it came to pastors of big churches, I longed to

receive some of the same respect they so obviously received. I noticed that a fair percentage of people at all levels in the Christian community respected pastors of big churches more than pastors of small ones. It was that way across the board. The way I saw it, they received the attention. They received the speaking engagements. They received all the renown, the perks, the fame, the big bucks, and even the respect of their superiors over pastors of small churches. I have observed this since my earliest days in the ministry, and it hasn't changed in all that time.

I had a brief brush with the success of having a big ministry in the first church I led as pastor. When I began pastoring the church, about sixty people attended. Within four years it grew to over four hundred. During that period in my life people got to know my name within the denomination I serve. My superiors at all levels began to treat me with greater respect. Often, when I was introduced to others for various reasons, I was presented as someone who was a pastor of a growing church and one of significant size. It was as if that fact earned me a badge of honor. I began to think, because of the way I was being treated, greater honor fell to pastors of larger churches, and the larger the church the greater the honor. I am not certain that I ever verbalized or penned this perception at that time, but there is no question I believed it.

So here I was with a second degree twenty years after receiving my first. I had a lot more information to use in my ministry. I had more letters behind my name. I achieved an accomplishment I could be proud of and one people were praising me for, but I hadn't learned a thing. I still thought big was better. Furthermore I just spent a boatload of money and put in thousands of burnout hours to verify that I wasn't any smarter than before.

All that was in my heart about big churches, successful ministries, and master's degrees seemed to be completely unrelated to the crises I was facing with the people in my church. My primary goal in going to school to get a degree was to ultimately have a bigger church. At the same time people in my church were going through intense personal crises that I needed to deal with. Then there was this crazy detective in the process of going over the edge who apparently chose me to dump his delusional garbage upon. I saw no relationship between the strains of events. They were all major time consumers that settled upon my life. I needed to put the blinders on and thereby block out the distractions. I just needed to get through everything without losing my own sanity.

A Diploma

The school from which I received my master's degree was an extension school attached to a seminary that hailed out of Tulsa, Oklahoma. I could receive my degree by mail or have it handed to me by the dean at the graduation ceremony in Tulsa. My wife convinced me to fly to Oklahoma to take part in the graduation ceremonies at the mother school. She said that it would be a memory I would want to have and insisted on being there with me for the occasion.

The Los Angeles riots of 1992, resulting from the Rodney King verdict, erupted just three days before my wife and I were to leave for Tulsa. As we traveled the 405 freeway to the Los Angeles airport, we became frighteningly aware of armed troops, military trucks, and other combat type vehicles stationed at various corners and checkpoints along the way. There were many large buildings that were burned to the ground. Opening our car windows revealed the strong smell of charred building remains.

My wife was very anxious about leaving our youngest son while we were in Tulsa, though he was going to be well attended to by a responsible caretaker. The events of the previous few days were terrifying. Hundreds of buildings were reduced to ashes and rubble. Businesses were looted. Innocent bystanders were hurt and killed. We sat glued to our television set in awe of the sheer pandemonium that took place just thirty minutes south of where we lived. Both of us felt very uneasy about leaving our family and home at that time.

The riots all took place in the Inglewood-Watts area of Los Angeles, but there were rumors circulating that at least one group of rioters were threatening to bring their destruction north over the pass into the San Fernando Valley where we lived. That was way too close to home, and my wife almost didn't go with me. The armed troops' presence near the airport certainly didn't help to calm her fears.

As our plane took off I began to recall the Rodney King beating from the videotape that hit every TV station in the country within a day or so after the event. The beating actually took place in the San Fernando Valley, only about a ten-minute drive from where we lived. The Lakeview Terrace exit off the 118 freeway near where the beating occurred was one I used many times. My family insisted on finding the location of the beating, so I took them to the spot the week after it took place. I acted investigative as if we were all on a first-time adventure, but I already checked out the site a few days earlier.

As our plane circled over the ocean and began heading east toward Oklahoma, I wondered, *Had events like the Rodney King beating played a part in influencing my detective counselee to begin to slip off the deep end? Perhaps he was there the night of the infamous flogging.* I tried to recall some of the eruptive statements he made to see if they might reveal his presence at the beating, but nothing seemed to fit.

I held a book in my hand but was having a hard time focusing on its content. I looked over at my wife. She was reading the airline magazine present at each seat. I knew from experience that she would much rather talk than read. I nudged her and suggested that I had something to tell her. I then betrayed the anonymity I promised and shared with her about the strange detective who came into my office on two occasions. She was intrigued and wanted to know more details about the man than I had information to give her. We both laughed at some of the antics he performed in my office. We then settled into the flight and resumed reading.

The graduation ceremony went well. I didn't trip and fall while ascending the steps to receive my diploma or while descending them. However, guilt for my betrayal got the best of me and I didn't mention the detective to Shirley again. We spent two short days there and returned home, much relieved to get back to our kids. Our ride from the airport to our house in the San Fernando Valley again revealed armed troops along the way and raised our anxieties a second time.

Yet we were relieved that the trip was without incident for us and for our children.

A diploma is a funny thing. Once I had it in my hands, I really didn't know what to do with it. I thought of displaying it, but in the end I put it in my desk drawer, and there it remains to this day. It isn't that I am ashamed of it. I just don't know for sure what it represents. Some say it's all about an accomplishment I can be proud of or evidence of increased knowledge. Others suggest it denotes a form of power. Still others maintain it stands for increased effectiveness. Yet I could name several ministers who have proven to be very effective who have lesser degrees than I.

Perhaps my uncertainty about what to do with my diploma and what it means is a reflection of my motivation to seek another degree in the first place. As I honestly ponder my innermost motives, I would have to admit that the driving force behind my seeking a higher degree was, as I suggested earlier in this chapter, I wanted to be *bigger*—a *bigger* person with a *bigger* church possessing *larger* amounts of acclaim. And though I have pursued that goal for many years in the ministry, deep down I know that there is something awry with that precise motivation.

Much of my ministry has been a kind of quest for answers concerning the idea that *bigger* is *better*. I didn't know it while I was on the quest. I merely went along serving and failing, ministering and blundering, shepherding and wandering, until one day something dawned on me. I was searching for answers to a question I never asked out loud or identified as a dilemma in my life. The question was: Is getting *bigger* a valid objective for a minister? It seemed to me that every minister

I knew pursued this objective without a hint of hesitation, including myself. Many of the discussions I had with other ministers pivoted around this very subject. No one seemed to carry any noticeable amounts of guilt for wanting to have bigger ministries. They just treated it as if it were the most natural and acceptable objective for all of us. Furthermore, the seminars and pastor's conferences I attended all seemed to possess the same general theme: "This is how to make your church *bigger*." I was being forced to consider whether any of it was rightly motivated.

I was in a wrestling match not unlike the one Jacob had with God in Genesis 32. Like Jacob, I was wrestling with God demanding a blessing. School was just another wrestling hold I was trying to impose upon God, and like Jacob, God would bless me. However, the mark of His blessing would not be anything like the blessing I sought. Instead I would go away with a puzzled look on my face, limping for all I was worth, and trying to figure out how that limp could possibly represent His blessing. But it would. It would take time for me to realize it, but it would represent His blessing.

CHAPTER 5

Silent Pain

I almost forgot about the crazy detective. It had been nearly three months since his last visit.

I looked up from my desk in time to see his car pull into our parking lot, although I didn't know it was his car, nor did I recognize him as the driver. I had not seen his automobile before. On his two previous visits he apparently parked down the street and walked to the church in an attempt to hide his identity. This time, however, he parked in our lot a long way from the front door and just sat there. Yet he was too far away for me to be able to recognize him.

At first I thought the person in the car was a lost traveler or a businessman who needed a quiet place to conclude some paperwork. People stopped in our parking lot for things like that all the time. I went back to my studies, unconcerned about which it might be.

About half an hour later I looked up again and the car with the driver inside was still there. I became a little more curious and peered more intentionally through my window at the car and driver until it dawned on me, *It's him. It's the weird detective.*

My first thought was, *How can I slip out of my office without him seeing me?*

It was not that I didn't care. I just did not have two hours, probably uncomfortable hours, to talk with him that day. I really did think he was nuts and that my being with him was a big waste of time. I knew he would never come to my church. His whole situation demanded that he remain anonymous. How could he and his family ever come to a church where he might be expected to become a name on a roll? And if he ever did come, what value could he be to the ministry? If someone could not contribute to a numbers increase in our church, I didn't have a whole lot of time for that person.

Just about the time I devised a plan to slip out of my office unnoticed, he exited his car and headed for the front door. I knew I couldn't leave with dignity at that point, so I sat back and waited for his knock. By that time I resolved that I was probably stuck with him for however long he was going to be there.

I don't know why I couldn't tell him *no*. I usually had little trouble turning people away with busyness or a previous engagement as an excuse. But for some reason, even though I may have had much work to do, I couldn't find it in my heart to tell him I was too busy to talk with him. Maybe I had the sense that though I assumed he was quite crazy, he labeled me as his only hope. Perhaps I merely didn't want to disappoint him. Maybe I didn't want to turn him away in the crazed condition in which he came to me. Yet when I would discover it was him, I wanted to get away. Go figure!

Whatever confused reasoning I followed in my mind, this day I opened my door to him again.

He came in quietly and sat down. He didn't say a word. When I asked him how he was, he remained silent. I suspected he had also been equally as silent in his car for the previous thirty minutes. I inquired about his feelings, but he wasn't about to speak. He just slumped in the chair and stared straight ahead with a blank look on his face. So we both just sat there.

We sat there for ten minutes…twenty minutes…thirty minutes…forty minutes…fifty minutes. What a trip! I felt awkward reading while he sat there. I felt awkward studying. I just felt awkward. So we continued to sit there.

What could be going on in a mind that needed me to listen but couldn't summon the words to speak; a mind that needed my answers, but couldn't muster the ability to ask the questions?

I watched the clock as the minutes ticked by. Absolutely no conversation took place. As he sat there I wondered about whether or not I was really doing him any good. I certainly had no thoughts that he was doing me any good. I thought about all the work I had to do, the sermons I had to write, the problems I had to solve, and the church I had to build. I thought about the presumptuousness with which he walked into my office, and did so without an appointment. I began to get angry, and I felt that what I was thinking was well-founded frustration toward him. *After all,* I also thought, *He's an absolute fruitcake.*

Finally, after about an hour, he spoke. In an even and controlled tone, as he continued to stare straight ahead, he said, "My name is David. That's all I can tell you."

My first thoughts in response were a bit flippant.

I thought, *Great! Now I know the crazy man's name.*

My next thought was more sensitive. *He's telling me his name. Could it be that he trusts me? This must be what they call a breakthrough.*

While still looking straight ahead he said, "I want to kill everyone."

My eyes opened wide and my thoughts instantly changed again. I thought, *Oh...my! This is it!*

My eyes frantically searched his belt and pocket area. I was mildly comforted to see that he probably wasn't toting a gun.

"What do you mean?" I asked, obviously nerved by his words.

He said, "I just hate everything I do and every person I have to deal with. I hate what my boss expects of me. I hate the neighborhoods I see every day. I hate the people on the streets. I hate the jerks I arrest. I hate my new partner. I even hate the guy I buy hotdogs from. If I could kill them all, it wouldn't hurt my feelings a bit." When he said this he looked over at me to see how I was going to respond.

I was a little taken aback, but mostly I was relieved his list didn't include my name.

I asked him, "What about your family? Do you want to kill them too?"

I watched his face turn from hard to soft. He then said gently, with what appeared to be a slight but tender smile forming on his face, "No, of course not. They are one of the few things in my life that keep me from cracking up completely."

"Listen," he said. "I know you think I'm off my rocker. You must feel like running for the hills when you see me coming. But please, just hang in there with me. Will you?"

I felt a little ashamed, because running for the hills was exactly what I wanted to do when I saw him coming.

He left a few minutes later. As I sat at my desk I watched through the window as he walked to his car, and I thought, *What kind of a disturbed soul could sit in silence for that length of time. What kind of pain must be fueling his rage and craziness?*

As I sat there I began to weep, because I instantly knew the answer to that question. You see, a year earlier I had also been brought to silence by the pain in my life, certainly not for the length of time David sat in quietness, but I was also unable to speak for a time. His pain had to do with whatever his daily routine imposed on him. My pain had to do with what I had to deal with on a daily basis as well. But mine was the pain of needing to have a *bigger* ministry.

I couldn't remember whether it was a conference, a breakfast meeting, or some other gathering I attended, but I remember *the words* well. The pastor who spoke *those words* was well respected, well intended, and well known in Christian circles. He told of the many people who asked him the same question over and over again.

They would ask him, "Why do you feel your church has grown?"

That particular day he reported to us the answer he gave them. His answer was humble and noble and plunged me into the deepest depression of my life.

He said, "I have no answer for why my church has grown. My only thought is that God, in His sovereignty, simply chose to bless us."

I left the gathering deep in thought concerning his words. The longer and harder I thought about them, the more discouraged I became. For days I pondered these noble words. I recall prolonged times where I would sit in my office in silence, unable to speak, unable to form words, because the words were too painful for me to utter.

One night around that time, my wife confronted me about my unusual but obviously depressed demeanor.

"What has been going on with you, anyway?" she finally asked me in our bedroom just before I was about to slip between the covers.

Instead of climbing into bed, I sat on its side and for several moments I could not speak. It wasn't that a dumb spirit possessed my tongue. It was that the thoughts in my head were too terrible to shape into words. Exposing the mental garbage I allowed to fester within me for several weeks to my wife who loved and respected me was an awful prospect to me. So I sat in silence, not for ninety minutes, but for several moments anyway. And yet I knew if I were going to get through it and find any resolve, I would have to turn my thoughts into verbiage.

So I began to speak the words that were in my heart.

I reminded her of the event where the respected minister spoke. I told her of his words, because she had not been with me to hear them. I told her of my weeks of processing his words and the infection of junky thinking I allowed to enter the process. I then told her about my final assessment of the whole thing, but I had not actually spoken the words or finalized my thoughts until I spoke them to my wife that night.

I said, "If he is right—and I have a sense he is—if it's true that God alone builds His church and therefore chooses to bless a church and pastor with growth, and since our church has seen no significant growth in the years we've been here, then it must be," I concluded, "God has simply chosen, for whatever reason, to *not* bless *us*."

I began to weep immediately after speaking those words. At that moment I felt complete rejection from God. I was convinced at that point in time that the God, who is believed to love everyone without exception, actually decided to make an exception. And that exception was me.

Crazy you say! Perhaps. But there I was, and I truly believed it. When I spoke the words it plunged me officially into a state of depression. It was *stinkin' thinkin'* for sure! But just the same, there I was deep in the heart of it.

My wife was so overcome with sympathy for me that she began to cry as well. She sat down beside me, held me, and we both wept together for several minutes before we went to bed in a king-sized funk.

I was in a depression for about three weeks. I would get up in the morning, say very little, and smile very little. I would go through the motions at work and get through church services the best I could.

As I sat there that day after David left, thinking through my own silence, I seemed to find a degree of respect for him and began to feel greater amounts of compassion for him and his apparent lunacy.

In future visits I still dreaded his coming, because he demanded my time on the spur of the moment, usually time I didn't have to give. But in a strange sort of way, I also began to look forward to his coming. He intrigued me—his craziness and all—and I began to wonder if God had a bigger purpose in sending this one man my way.

Chapter 6

Mortality

David never made appointments. I surmised after his second visit that it was because he feared if he were to set an appointment, I might have an officer or some law enforcement person at my church waiting for him to arrive. He would be found out and that would be the end of that.

And always there would be enough time between his drop-ins to cause me to forget about him altogether, and even consider the prospect that I wouldn't see him again. Usually a minimum of two months would pass between visits. Once I didn't see him for six months. So each time he came, it was a surprise. And each time he came, what he managed to communicate to me was also a surprise.

I remember well the day he told me about his partner. I remember partly because he didn't exactly come ready to bear his soul. I had to coax it out of him as if we were playing a game of charades. I remember it also because it was my first clear glimpse of what set off the time bomb in David's soul in the first place.

On that day I recall feeling someone standing in front of my window. I looked up, and there he was.

My first impression was, *Great! There goes another two hours.* But those feelings fizzled quickly as I watched his antics.

His back was to me, and he just stood there. He stayed in that spot for about ten minutes. Then he leaned toward the door and reached for the knob, but instead of coming in, he stepped back to his original place in front of my window, all the while with his back to me. Five minutes or so later with his back still aimed in my direction and against my window, he repeated his previous move toward the door and again stepped back to where he was in front of my window.

I almost laughed out loud. I wondered, *He must know I can see him. Is he aware of how foolish he looks?* At that thought I knew he probably wasn't, and I wondered what pain he must be going through.

I almost went to his rescue just to help him along, but figured the struggle he was having was one he needed to work through himself. So I left him alone. I went on working though I was significantly distracted by the apparent life-and-death battle going on outside my window. Finally he made a bold lunge for the door, turned the handle, and walked into the outside office.

Since there were no windows between the front office and mine, I couldn't see him as he entered. Once he came into the outer office, I fully expected him to knock on my door but heard nothing. No knocking…no breathing…no mumbling or fumbling…no sounds at all. He just stood there the same way he stood in front of my window for what seemed to be forever. It was at least another ten minutes before he finally knocked. Needless to say, I didn't make much progress on my work during that time.

At the sound of the taps I rose from my desk, stepped to the door, and opened it. David was standing straight and tall at attention in front of my door as if he mustered the courage to stand toe to toe before his army commander and face a court martial.

He looked into my eyes and asked, "Can we talk today?" I almost chuckled, because it seemed he was completely oblivious to the fact that he put on a show for me in front of my window for the past half hour. Truly he was in his own twisted world of pain. Yet he spoke as if he were on a mission to divulge a most crucial bit of information to me.

Crucial it was; and tell me he would, but not in simple words.

He walked in and sat down. He squatted down into my guest chair in what almost looked to be a fetal position. I thought, *What happened to the bravery with which he stood before my door only a moment before?* He sat straight, facing me, but his legs were tight together and folded up under his chair, crossed at the ankles. He put his hands in his lap in what looked to be a reverent or submitted pose and hung his head as if he were afraid to look up.

I waited for him to speak, but the struggle I observed earlier was now manifesting itself on his face and in his efforts to formulate words. He was attempting to talk, but it wasn't working. His lips seemed to be trying to form words, but he couldn't bring his vocal chords to utter the sounds. When the sounds refused to come he would pull his lips back to their nonspeaking position on his face, pursed and closed.

After a few minutes, in an effort to coax him along, I asked, "David, what do you want to tell me today?"

It didn't help. It was probably insensitivity on my part to try and move him along, but I continued to pose questions, hoping something I would ask might help to loose his tongue. "Do you want to tell me something about your family?" I queried.

He closed his eyes and, with his head still lowered, he shook his head no.

I thought for a few minutes while he remained silent, and then asked, "Does it have to do with someone close to you?"

I knew it wasn't best for a counselor to push clients too hard, but I couldn't see going through another hour of silence as we had the last time he came. I never claimed to be a good counselor, and I still wasn't sure how I felt about David's visits anyway. The way I saw it, for the sake of not wasting another significant quantity of time, I would continue to prod him. I seemed to have gotten a response with my last question.

He looked up at me and shook his head yes.

"Who?" I asked.

He looked at me and began to mouth words that wouldn't come again, until finally he whispered, "My... my...my...partner."

And then he began to cry. I never saw a tear from him before, but that day he was crying right out loud and kept on crying. His crying turned into guttural sobs with no hint of concluding. I wanted to reach over and touch him, but I wasn't sure what kind of a response I might receive— a lurch away in angry protest or a bolt for the exit in disgust. So I sat behind my desk and just tried to sympathize.

And I knew instinctively from listening to him wail that

something tragic happened to his partner, whom, I surmised, must have been his old partner. I also knew that this partner had been more than a partner; he was David's dear and trusted friend.

I waited for his sobbing to subside, then I asked, "He was hurt…or worse…wasn't he?"

Looking down, David shook his head yes.

I passed him a box of Kleenex, which was on the bookshelf behind me, but David didn't respond. I waited a few more moments and asked, "He was more than a partner, wasn't he? He was your buddy…your friend."

Again, with his head still looking down, David nodded yes.

At this point I was finished with prodding. I sat there and waited for David to talk, which didn't take long. And once the *proverbial dam* broke next would come *the flood*.

David reached up, grabbed a Kleenex out of the box, blew his nose, and began to speak slowly and deliberately.

"It happened a little more than two years ago; about a year before I came to you. It was supposed to be a routine drug bust. We worked the case through our informants for a long time—three or four months, I think."

I looked for him to lose it again, but he didn't. He went on telling the story in a slow and even tone.

"The apartment was off an alley in a nasty part of town. One thing or another happens in this area almost every day; shootings, overdoses, rapes, you name it. I knocked on the door, but there was no answer, so I turned the knob. It was unlocked, so I pushed open the door. Steve—that was my partner—was right behind me. And behind him we had more backup."

I listened with a sympathetic facial expression, but I was on the edge of my seat.

David went on, "The whole place was dark and dingy. It was a back-alley apartment, and it was ugly. I remember there was a single lamp lit with what might have been a forty-watt bulb. But it seemed really quiet and sort of peaceful. We are taught that we are never supposed to let down our guard, but everything seemed so harmless."

I could feel David reliving the story maybe for the first time since it happened, and I was right there with him.

"When we stepped into the place," David continued, "there were two guys sitting on a dirty old couch. One of them was black; the other Hispanic. I raised my gun and said 'This is a bust,' but they never moved. They just sat there. They were really wasted. I think one of them finally said something like, 'Bummer,' and the other one said, 'Yeah.'"

David paused for a moment, and I could feel his thoughts wandering off, probably back to the incident itself. In a few seconds he shook his head as if to ward off his wandering recollections so he could come back to the present.

He went on, "Steve said, 'Looks like everything is in control here. I'll check down the hall.'"

Again David stopped to let his mind wander. But this time, I could feel him beginning to breathe harder. I saw in his face a searching that seemed to be trying to find something more than what actually happened. It was as if he were reenacting the whole incident and rethinking what he did or didn't do or say, all at the same time.

In a few moments he continued, "I don't know why

I didn't tell him to be careful. And I don't know why I didn't suspect any danger."

Breathing harder now, David went on, "Steve entered the hallway. It wasn't much of a hall really, just a short passage to the end, where there was another door. I could see him out of the corner of my eye. He was too relaxed...too casual. I sensed it then, but I didn't say anything. I still don't know why I didn't say anything."

I wasn't sure whether I should let David continue. It felt almost as if he were about to disassociate. Though he was telling me the story, I wasn't sure he was fully aware that I was there. The tension he displayed scared me. Just the same, I restrained myself from interrupting.

With his teeth gritted now, David continued, "I was still holding my gun up and looking at the two druggies on the front room couch when I heard Steve kick open the door. Not hard...just with his toe. The door must have been slightly cracked open."

David took a deep breath in an attempt to gather himself, and said, "I heard Steve yell 'No!'"

Then David stopped. I could see he didn't want to say the next words. I remember thinking, *How is he staying seated?* Then I looked at his hands and saw that they were gripping the arms of my guest chair with what appeared to be destructive force.

He then took about three very long and deep breaths and said, "Just then a shot went off." He stared straight ahead with a blank look on his face for perhaps ten seconds, which seemed more like ten hours.

Finally he said, "And then there was another shot."

David looked at me, and I stared back at him. There were tears streaming from both eyes. He swallowed hard and said rather calmly, "He never saw it coming. The scum was standing right in front of the door. He must have been waiting for Steve."

He paused for another moment and said, "The scum was also a coward. He waited for Steve to open the door; then he shot Steve straight through the forehead, turned the gun on himself, and pulled the trigger again. We couldn't even take the guy to court."

I found myself fighting back my own tears without much success.

When he composed himself, David stood up, turned around, and walked over to the window. While looking outside he said, "I have so much hate in me. It's so deep down I don't know if God could dig it out...let alone forgive me for it. The problem is I don't know who to hate. For a while I hated the guy who killed Steve. Then I hated God for letting it happen. Then I hated myself. I figured since I was lead between us, I must have done something wrong. I still feel like I must be to blame, because I should have said something. But pretty much now, I don't hate anybody specific, I just hate."

For the longest time I didn't know what to say. I could see David lightly sobbing, while still looking out the window and sniffling every few seconds. I hurt for him, but mostly, I was stunned.

Finally I asked, "Am I the first one you've told?"

"No, of course not," he said. "I told it at least ten times during the investigation."

Then he paused, stretched his head up high, and said, "But I told it like a good cop, with a straight face and attention to detail. You learn to do that when you have to. That's the only way to keep your job."

David was still standing and looking out the window. He stayed that way for several uncomfortable moments. I didn't know what to say, and David chose not to speak, so I sat and he stood, neither of us saying a word.

As he stood there I thought about his partner, Steve. I didn't know what he looked like or what kind of person he was, but it seemed possible to me that he was even more than just David's buddy. He may have been David's only friend. I knew enough about people's personalities to assess that David was an extreme introvert. Introverts seldom have many friends, but usually have at least one, at the most a few. It seemed very probable that Steve had been David's one and only friend; the one person he could talk to, confide in, and help him remain sane in the midst of stresses.

Furthermore, Steve's absence was a tension source all by itself—a very serious one. David was filled with hatred because his friend and comrade was gone. So his stress-venting mechanism actually became the source of his stress. This was no doubt creating a confusion that was having a disastrous impact on David. It confused me just thinking about it. One thing was certain: a key accountability aid in David's life vanished, and he was suffering great anguish because of it.

I was with David for nearly two hours, and I wasn't sure if we were finished. It seemed, however, as if the subject we discussed contained the weight of the world and needed some debriefing. But I wasn't sure that I, or David, had enough strength to carry on that day.

Finally he turned around and in keeping with my thoughts, he said, "I think I'm done for today."

David thanked me for listening, shook my hand, and left. I watched him as he walked across the parking lot. His back was to me as he walked away, but I could see the hurt on his face just the same. Halfway to his car, he stopped and stood for several seconds. Though his back was to me, I could see him lift his hands to his head and gently pound the palms of his two closed fists to both sides of his forehead seven, maybe eight, times. Then he lowered his hands to his sides, took a deep breath, and shuffled off to his car.

I thought, *What excruciating pain must be in that heart of his!* Then my mind went to the story he just told me. I picked up a pen and wrote on a stray slip of paper three words: *hatred...symptoms...upbringing.* I wrote David's name at the top and slipped it into my counseling files. I knew if David ever came back again, as he allowed, we would need to delve into these three subjects. And I figured if the pain of that day's session was great for David, the pain in future sessions, especially as we addressed these issues, would be even greater. I wasn't sure I was looking forward to it.

CHAPTER 7

Symptoms

I was beginning to look for David as I shopped in stores and drove down streets; not always, just when I thought about it. I guess I was hoping to see him in a normal setting to help me to be convinced he was normal, though I felt deep in my heart he probably wasn't. I wasn't sure whether or not he lived nearby, but I thought he might. Sometimes I would see people who looked similar. I would follow them with my eyes to see if any would turn out to be David, but none did.

Mysteriously, David never came to talk to me when someone else was around; never when there was another visitor, church member, or even so much as a mailman at the church. I surmised this was of David's own doing. I thought it must be that he watched carefully to be sure no one else was around before he came to the church door. But even that theory seemed far-fetched because he was always with me for at least two hours. The chance of his being with me for that length of time each time he came, and never once encountering someone else from our church or a visitor, was almost impossible. Yet that was the case.

I remember once thinking, *If I ever had to prove in order*

to save my life that a detective named David existed whom I counseled from time to time, I'd be a goner. There were no witnesses. That is why David, and my connection with him, was so mysterious. I can't remember when it was, but at a certain point I began to entertain the possibility that he was an angel. I just wasn't sure that an angel could act as David acted and cuss as David cussed.

I was recuperating from a thumb injury the next time David came by. Those who are acquainted with me also know I have a propensity toward severing my digits.

In my first church we decided to remodel our main auditorium. We organized work crews every night for a week, from Sunday afternoon through Saturday evening. Our goal was to have the whole job concluded before the next Sunday. We had the project planned down to a science. The materials, workers, and tools were ready to go for every night. On Tuesday evening, however, the work came to a grinding halt when I took a skill saw to my left hand and promptly severed an inch off the end of my little finger. I was taken to the hospital, and, during a late night surgery, the recovered tip was sewn back on.

It was a traumatic night for me, but it wasn't long before the jokes began to fly. "Pastor Chris left his blood on the altar." "Chris and power tools don't get along." "Whatever you do, don't let him touch a saw." Not to mention, I must have heard every stub joke in existence.

I thought departing from that church would leave my reputation behind; however, when I sliced a significant amount of flesh from the side of my left thumb with a paper cutter, somehow my reputation returned, and the jokes with it.

Anyway, I had a large, cumbersome bandage on my left thumb and was fumbling with paper over the copy machine when David came through the door of our front office. I leaned back and looked around the doorway when I heard the front door open and saw David standing there.

As usual my first thoughts weren't enthusiastic. I thought, *Oh, boy! How am I going to do this today?*

But I said, "Just a minute, David. Why don't you go into my office and sit down. I'll be with you shortly."

Since the accident happened only the day before, and in spite of the pain medication I was taking, my thumb was still throbbing. Consequently, I didn't feel very alert. But in the ministry, with unalterable deadlines coming rapid-fire every Sunday, and on-call emergencies blindsiding me when I least expect, I often don't have the luxury of saying to people, "Sorry, I can't help you today."

That week not only did my sermon receive "not-so-alert" attention, but it was also apparent that David was going to have to settle for a little mental dullness from me as well.

I walked into my office, trying to hide my left hand, while offering my right for a handshake. But David noticed the very large white ball of gauze on my thumb anyway.

"What'd ya do to your thumb?" he asked.

I responded in jest, "Oh, I thought I'd trim off a little excess skin with the paper cutter."

David thought for a moment and said, "You know, paper cutters are supposed to be for cutting paper, not thumbs."

He looked at me and smiled while I chuckled back, and I thought, *He's joking. That has to be a good sign.*

I was in pain, but as our smiles faded, I was reminded

of the pain David left my office with about three months before. Then I remembered the three words I wrote on a piece of scrap paper and slipped into my file the last time he was here.

I asked, "How are you doing today, David?" as I leaned to my left and opened my desk file drawer. I reached with my left hand into the file. As I did I realized I wasn't going to have the dexterity to retrieve it with that hand, so I made a few awkward moves to spin my chair around to enable me to thumb through the file with my good hand.

David began talking, oblivious to the awkwardness I was engaged in and unaware of my seeming inattentiveness. But I heard his every word.

He began by saying, "I'm a little scared."

Though I was fidgeting, he got my attention. I glanced up to see if he noticed my awkward movements, but he was looking at the floor. I continued to search for the tiny piece of paper.

He went on to say, "When I told you last time about Steve's death, I didn't tell you what was really bothering me."

I was already frustrated because of my clumsy effort to get into my file, but I continued to listen, because his words had my complete interest. Yet once I turned around so I could search with my right hand, I couldn't locate the piece of paper I was looking for.

David kept on talking just the same. "About three months after Steve was killed, I started doing crazy things. They gave me a new partner, but I don't like him at all. No reason really; he's just not Steve. So I couldn't talk to him."

"Couldn't talk about what?" I asked as I looked for the

illusive piece of paper. "What did you feel you needed to talk about?"

"I think it's called—self-mutilation," he said.

I heard it, and my attention was significantly captured, but I was also extremely frustrated trying to find the piece of paper. I was about to give up when it finally appeared. I grabbed it, closed the drawer, and placed it on the desk in front of me.

By then I knew one of the words on the paper was indeed going to be the subject matter of our discussion that day. I got settled at my desk, placed the paper in front of me, and grabbed a pen. As David continued to talk, I put the point of the pen to the paper and circled the middle word written on it—*symptoms*.

I actually experienced indications of a slight adrenaline rush, probably from the shock of hearing what he just said and from anticipation of what we may get into in our discussion as a result. What kinds of things would I be hearing that day?

"What do you mean by *self-mutilation*?" I asked. I was gravely concerned, but I tried not to show it. By then my distraction concluded, so he had my undivided attention.

He swallowed hard and said, "I think I went nuts. I mean you have to be nuts when you do that sort of thing, right?"

"What were you doing to yourself?" I asked. But the thoughts foremost in my mind were, *This is getting way out of my league. How am I going to help this man?* I felt extremely inadequate, yet I knew I was in the thick of it just the same. I was his "chosen one," so I settled myself in and prepared for a harrowing tale.

By the time the dust settled that day, I had a pretty clear picture of why David was so afraid and why he ever showed up at my door in the first place.

Before Steve's death David was already numb from the constant bad news he encountered every day, but when his partner and best friend fell, his whole perspective changed. Before, he was able to compartmentalize the bad news and leave it at work. He was also able to rationalize the depravity as something he and his fellow officers were making a difference in over time. But after the death of his comrade, nothing made sense anymore. The thoughts all just seemed to get jumbled together after that.

To add to the confusion in his head was anger...intense anger. He wanted to obliterate his companion's slayer, but couldn't for obvious reasons. He was unable to approach every street situation he encountered after that with a civil mind. Every day he felt himself slipping further and further away from normalcy.

It wasn't so much an outward thing. He didn't throw things or abuse the criminals he arrested. Nor did he explode out of control for all to see. His new partner didn't think him a raving maniac. It was all inward, and that, no doubt, aggravated the problem.

He couldn't share it with his wife. It became way too ugly for that. He already told me that it would escalate her fears and intensify her nagging for him to quit the force altogether. She may even go to his captain herself. So he kept it all inside, becoming more and more cynical within and more hateful by the minute.

Then the story got really strange. At times he would stop

the car, order his new partner to stay in the vehicle, and disappear into an alley. There he would sit down behind a dumpster and just cry, or he would stand and stare at a puddle or a corner for several minutes. Sometimes he would pound his head on the side of a building or take a piece of metal and scrape himself until he bled. Then he would come to himself and return to the car with some lie about meeting an informant, but he was very careful to say nothing about the insanity he felt himself becoming more and more enslaved to every day.

He held all this inside for several months. He didn't tell his wife, his new partner, or anyone on his precinct. He figured he could handle it by himself…until one day.

There was a girl, a heroine addict he met in his dealings. He started out using her for information. Later, however, he learned her sources weren't trustworthy, but he developed a soft place in his heart for her. It wasn't because of any romantic interest he had in her. She just reminded him of his sister. The girl's name was Julie.

He started to take care of Julie. From time to time he would bring her a burger and some fries. If he saw her on the street, without fail, he would pull his car up next to her and talk to her for as long as she seemed interested. She was the only bright spot in his world. He thought in his own twisted way, *If everything falls apart…if the whole world goes to hell…if I could just save Julie, all would be OK.*

Even that hope seemed to be fading though, because more and more, when he pressed her about her lifestyle she would get extremely upset and yell at him to mind his own business. Then she would walk away in disgust.

On the day he decided to talk to someone about his craziness, Julie overdosed and was brought to the hospital. He found out through a friend of hers in the neighborhood. He went straight to the person he expected was her supplier, held a gun to his head, and told him if he ever sold her as much as another hit, he was a dead man. Apparently, detectives made these kinds of threats periodically, but this one was different. He knew the crazed emotions inside his head were out of control. He sensed at that moment that if he were to pull the trigger, he would feel no remorse at all.

I lifted my eyes and watched David carefully as he unfolded this part of the story. I felt great apprehension, because, at that point, I wondered if he was about to tell me that he did shoot the man.

I wanted to break in and clarify, "Did you? Did you pull the trigger?" If he shot the man, my time with him was over. I knew if there were a dead drug dealer out there somewhere because of David's craziness, I would have to go to the authorities. But he went on without skipping a beat, and I let him.

Later that day he screeched the car to a halt, ran into an alley, and began to pound his head against the wall and scream. He screamed so loudly his partner heard him and came running to help, fearing David was in danger. David actually had blood on his forehead from banging his head against the bricks. He collected himself though, and told his partner he tripped and hit his head on the alley floor and was so angry about it he began to scream. His partner seemed to buy it, but the detective from that moment on knew he was in trouble.

He told me that when a cop begins to lose it, there is no place for solace. You can't get a break from the corruption to recoup. You face it every day. Every assignment exposes you to new and ghastly variations of disgust, and when you cross a line emotionally as he had, going out on the streets is like heading into a den of lions.

The sights he encountered, the depravity he observed, and the corruption he ran into the next week seemed to be unbearable. He saw abused children, drug overdoses, gang murders, and the like in environments that would make the ghetto look like a neighborhood in the suburbs.

He pulled his alley routine once more and was spotted by a couple of street cops. They heard him while he was having one of his episodes behind a dumpster. When they yelled at him from the end of the alley, rather than identifying himself and risk being reported as a cop engaging in peculiar behavior, he decided to run.

The beat cops gave a good chase down the alley and around several corners. In the end, however, he eluded them and caught a cab. He then had the driver deliver him to the burger stand around the corner from his precinct and called his partner from his office phone. His story to his partner about what happened again calmed suspicions, but in his mind, he was about to crack.

That night, rather than go home, he checked into a hotel. He called his wife and told her he had to be on a surveillance assignment for a couple of days, but he would check in.

He never left the hotel room to eat, take a walk, or buy a soda. He simply sat, lay, paced, and stared at the walls for two days and nights. His only contacts with the outside world were with his wife to allay her fears and with his precinct to call in sick two days.

It was after the hotel incident that he began to physically look for someone to talk to about his craziness.

As I listened to his story I was filled with understanding, not about what was wrong with David, but about why he was so scared.

I was filled with awe. I read about people who caused themselves personal harm, but never directly encountered the problem before. I could tell David was hoping for some miracle bit of wisdom to roll off my lips concerning why he would attempt to hurt himself, but I had none. I shared what little knowledge I had on the subject with him, but wasn't sure it was beneficial. I think what helped him more was that he finally had the opportunity to tell someone.

When David left that day I recalled the incident when I had my mishap with a skill saw and severed the end of my little finger. For the longest time, people kidded me that I was subconsciously trying to punish myself for secret sins I was committing. As I pondered this recollection I thought, *Oh, no. Now that I've hurt my hand again, people are going to start teasing me about that, just like before.* As I thought about this I smiled, but my grin faded as I considered the implications of self-inflicted pain for David. The harassment I received was a joke. David's situation was serious, and I didn't have a clue as to how to help him.

CHAPTER 8

Hatred

The church is a problem magnet. It attracts all manner of issues in people's lives that are shrouded in all manner of disguises. Sitting all alone at the top of the problem list is hatred.

Over the years in the ministry, I have encountered an incredible amount of hatred. One would think the church should attract love, but it makes sense that the destructiveness of hatred would be drawn to the church's love, because it subconsciously hopes the church will be able to solve the problems its hatred produces. At times it does, but sometimes it doesn't.

Hatred can manifest itself in many things including broken relationships, schism between people, roots of bitterness, mistrust, spite, revenge, and anger. I have seen anger and hatred imbed itself so completely into the lives of certain people that it would take a miracle of enormous proportions for that person to identify it, let alone own it, and then extract it. I have encountered people in my ministry with such intense anger issues that I was surprised they hadn't yet killed anyone. And I fully expected that at some point in the near future they would.

That is why I was concerned when David spoke clearly to me in an earlier session about the disdain he saw burning in his own heart. From my experience I was relatively sure a great deal of the craziness that resulted in David's self-hurt was probably related to the hatred he felt.

A month or so before David showed up for his next session, God allowed an anger issue to present itself in my own life and ministry. You have already read about my struggles with ministry increase. Those struggles came to the surface and ultimately to a head during the time I spent in Northridge, California. Throughout my tenure there it seemed that time after time, growth and church size challenges presented themselves, demanding that I confront them face-to-face. One such incident occurred right around the time when the details of David's hatred surfaced.

Prior to his next visit, a financial crisis occurred in our church, demanding that we lay off a staff member. Wanting to be fair, we took extensive effort to make recommendations and phone calls and to help that person secure another ministry position. We were satisfied that we had done right by him.

Following this staff member's departure, perhaps six weeks later, we learned that his initial reaction to the layoff announcement angered him so much that he began to say bad things about our church's leadership and me. His talk turned into a cancer of discord, and by the time it came to a head, we were at risk of losing fifty people—nothing short of a devastating church split in a church our size. During those six weeks I sensed there was a problem; I just didn't know the source. For forty-five days I gathered facts and talked to families in an effort to get to the bottom of the uprising so that I might be able to fix it. During that time I began to suspect that this staff member was at the bottom of the problems, but I tried to maintain an understanding attitude, not wanting to jump to judgmental conclusions. Yet when all the facts were gathered, it was apparent he systematically communicated with certain families in our church in a calculated effort to hurt our fellowship as severely as he could once he left. He did so even though we made special effort to help him obtain a new job.

The combination of betrayal while I was trying to help him and the looming probability of seeing the fabric of our church ripped apart created a significant anger issue in my heart. Through meetings with the at-risk families, we were able to retain about half of them, but we still lost about twenty-five people, and the whole incident left a sour taste in my mouth and considerable feelings of frustration in my heart toward this person.

David walked through our parking lot heading my way, obviously filled with hatred, and I sat at my desk watching him come, so filled with hatred myself that I didn't at all qualify to counsel him on the matter.

When David entered and sat down, we engaged in small talk for a few minutes. I remembered the tiny slip of paper I inserted into my counseling files that had the three subjects written on it. My thumb was thoroughly healed by then and no longer cumbersome, so I found it quickly. While we were still chitchatting, I set it in front of me. I then took a pen and circled a second word on the piece of paper, and when the conversation quieted I asked, "David, how are you doing with things since our last time together?"

I thought he might want me to remind him of what we talked about, because it had been more than four months since he last came by and since our last discussion about his self-inflicted injuries. He didn't hesitate even a second, as if that discussion occurred only the day before.

"I haven't been doing any more of that cutting stuff to myself since last time," he said. "Maybe I just needed to say it to someone, but I...I still think I must be nuts."

His head was down as if he were both discouraged and afraid to look at me.

I said, "You know, David, there are a lot of things you're *not* doing anymore. You're *not* screaming. You're *not* pacing back and forth in my ultra-roomy office. You're *not* crawling on the floor or jumping up and down. And now you tell me you're *not* scraping yourself or pounding your head against the wall anymore. That sounds like progress to me. Maybe you're even getting better."

He kept his head down. I wasn't sure whether my words struck a nerve of hope in him or not. I watched him for a few more seconds and then continued, "I'd like to ask a few questions about something I think might be related. Is it OK?"

He shrugged his shoulders and said, "I guess."

With that permission I paused for a moment to give myself a chance to think. I wanted to choose my next words carefully. Finally I said, "David, a few sessions back, you said you hated everyone—God, your new partner, even your hot-dog vender. Do you remember saying that?"

I waited for a response from David, but as soon as I spoke the word *hate*, a light turned on inside of me. I realized at that moment that that was exactly what I was doing right then. I was deep in the heart of hatred. I didn't have time or occasion to deal with it right then, but I knew I would need to address it at some point after David left. Up until then I never actually called what I felt *hatred*. *Righteous indignation*, maybe; *justified disapproval*, perhaps; but not *hatred*. It caused me uneasiness, because I enjoyed what I felt toward this former staff member, and I felt justified feeling it. Furthermore, I wasn't sure I was willing just yet to give those feelings up.

David thought about what I asked him, and in a few moments, he lifted his head, looked at me, and said inquisitively, "Yeah, I guess I do. So?"

After David's last session with me I quizzed a licensed counselor who attended our church about hatred. I asked her if she thought intense hatred over a long period of time could cause someone to want to injure himself or herself.

She said, "Of course. Anything that would cause guilt could compel someone over time to do all kinds of self-destructive things, the least of which would be physical punishment." She also said, "Hatred is one of the most powerful emotions there is, but do you know that there are a couple of emotions that usually occur before hatred?"

I was a bit clueless, but I tried to look knowledgeable.

She went on, "Anger usually happens before hatred. If a person is intensely angry for a long time, it isn't uncommon for that anger to eventually turn to bitterness or hatred, but before anger always comes hurt."

When I finished talking to the counselor, I went straight to my office, wrote it down, and attached it to the slip of paper that contained the three words: *symptoms, hatred,* and *upbringing.* It read, "Hurt causes anger…anger causes hatred…and hatred can cause self-destructiveness." I had it in front of me as I talked to David that day. Truthfully, I wasn't sure I knew what to do with the information.

I went on, "Do you think these feelings of hatred inside of you began at the time of Steve's death or did they begin before that, perhaps a long time before that?"

When someone has deep issues like David did and goes to a professional counselor, it customarily takes months, even years, of weekly counseling sessions for that person to work through those difficulties in order to acquire a sense of wholeness. It takes this kind of time, because people are reluctant to delve into their past or their psyche; it is too painful and fragile. Self-esteem is too easily damaged, so it usually takes an enormous amount of painstaking therapy in order to help someone reach a semblance of normalcy.

It was different with David, perhaps not at the beginning, but at a certain point. It was as if David knew what his problems were and precisely what he needed to do in order to work through them. It seemed as if he were on a mission to get normal and just needed someone he could talk to who could guide him through the process.

I listened as he talked for the next hour.

Anger issues like David's create a maze that people take years to feel their way through, but David bounded through his maze as if he had been that way before and memorized the exit route. It was apparent David thought hard about these issues. He certainly had plenty of time to do so between sessions. When I opened the door he boldly walked through it.

"I have always cared about people," he began. "I used to feel sorry for the nerdy kids who were picked on by the bullies in high school. I didn't rush to their rescue, but I felt genuinely sorry for them. I remember one time I tried to help a kid who was tripped by a bully and dropped all his books. Not only did the two friends I was with think I was weird for caring about him, the kid I tried to help told me to "buzz off" as well. I think he must have thought that I was mocking him."

"When I got hired onto the police force, I knew right away I was going to have trouble, because I couldn't get people's faces off my mind. I would take them with me wherever I went, including home. I would wake up from a sound sleep with nightmares that included the faces I saw of poor kids or teenage prostitutes or battered women."

"I could never do what those in the police academy said we should do. They told us, 'You have to develop a hard exterior, and you have to leave it where you saw it—on the streets.' I could never do that. When I talked to other cops concerning how bad I felt about some of the things I saw, they would give me a strange look and say, 'What are you, some kind of Mother Teresa? Just let it go.' After a while, I got the idea that I was the only one who felt like I did and that others were of the opinion that anyone who thought the way I did was a little strange. So I quit talking to people about the things I felt."

"Steve was a 'by-the-book' cop. He wasn't cold, but he saw the wisdom in having a thick skin toward the things we saw. He would always scold me when I talked sympathetically about people, partially, I guess, because he was trying to protect me, and partially because the pain would get to him too. So I quit talking to him as well. In fact I quit talking to anyone about it."

"Did you ever talk to your wife about it?" I asked, knowing my wife is an excellent sounding board.

"Are you kidding? Susan—" he paused for a moment as if he realized he gave me more information than he intended. Then he continued, probably thinking it was too late, but more than likely the information was safe with me anyway. "Susan freaks out when I come home with a band aid on my finger. How could I talk to her about the problems I run into on the streets? We'd have two basket cases in the family."

As David talked I saw a simple but obvious pattern unfolding. Before me sat a man who truly cared about the needs of people and one who had been plunged into an environment that was overflowing with some of the most extreme problems you could find. Then he was unable to adapt the conventional coping mechanisms taught him for allowing those problems to roll off his back. But there wasn't one person in the whole world he could talk to about it, and it was that way for several years.

David went on, "At some point, the compassion I felt for people started to turn into anger for the causes of their problems. Instead of feeling sorry for the addict, I felt anger for the pusher. Instead of feeling sympathy for the abused kid, I wanted to strangle his parents. I suppose I started to hate God for allowing it as well, but it wasn't normal feelings of anger I felt. Many cops would express anger for those kinds of things too, but I would take my anger with me wherever

I went. I would feel it deep inside of me. I found myself actually rehearsing scenarios of how I would kill the pushers and abusive parents so I could get away with it. As I would rehearse these plots, I would seethe with anger toward these people. At some point I remember feeling such intense anger toward an abusive mother; I took a paper clip on my desk, bent it open and scratched myself with it so deeply it drew blood. I hurt myself, because I couldn't hurt her. I remember that the shock of the pain I felt and the blood I saw dripping from my arm caused my hatred toward her to subside. I guess in a strange way I interpreted that as feeling better."

As I listened, I was astounded at what I heard. Not only did David unravel years of pain seemingly all by himself, he told me harrowing tales, the likes of which I never imagined. I wanted to break in, excuse myself, run outside, and scream; but I knew I couldn't. I sat there and listened, forcing back the tears and emotion I felt.

When a break in David's monologue presented itself, I asked him, "Can you identify a time when you first noticed that your concern for people started to turn into hatred for their abusers?"

As I asked the question, I thought it was a dubious question, and David probably had no idea when a transition like that could have occurred. But to my surprise David answered with bold certainty, "I know exactly when it occurred. It was about twelve years ago when the Freeway Killer was stalking his victims."

When he said this, I almost fell off my seat, because I too had an emotional tie to that infamous character in Los Angeles history.

CHAPTER 9

Sources of Trouble

In 1980, approximately eleven years before this odd detective initially came into my life and while I was leading my first church in South Gate, California, a young man who attended our church then became a victim of a widely publicized serial killer in southern California. The young man's name was Sean King. His killer, it was presumed, was William Bonin, who was captured in late spring of the same year.

I'll never forget the day Ray, who oversaw our youth ministry, called and told me the shocking news. It was in late July of 1980.

"Do you remember Sean King?" Ray asked.

I said, "Sure, I do. Good looking, blonde-haired kid…about fourteen. But I haven't seen him in church lately. Is everything all right?"

"Well, that's why I am calling," Ray said. "I received a call from his mother and Sean has been missing for several months and is feared dead. They have information that causes them to believe he was a victim of the Freeway Killer. His mom is extremely upset and wants to talk to you."

Sean was of average height for a fourteen-year-old. His

soft, dirty blonde hair was almost perfectly straight and hung stylishly over his collar. He had an innocent look about him and a gentle demeanor that went well with his appearance. Reportedly, Sean was the type of young man with the kind of appearance that the Freeway Killer seemed to seek out.

It seemed that on the night of his disappearance, Sean called his mother from a friend's house to say he was headed for a bus stop on Firestone Boulevard on the east side of Downey, California, to catch a ride home. The Freeway Killer was a known and feared perpetrator, but at the time Sean disappeared no one knew that this terrifying serial killer actually held his residence in Downey. Ironically, on that horrific night, Sean's mother insisted he call her to let her know that he was all right. It was just after ten thirty at night when he reached her, and it was the last time she spoke to him. Apparently, as Sean waited for the bus that night, the killer pulled up next to the bus stop. He proceeded to capture enough of Sean's trust to draw the young man near his vehicle so he could snatch him. Sean was never again seen alive.

After hanging up with Ray, I called Mrs. King and scheduled a night to visit her.

I don't remember a time when I felt a greater sense of sorrow and despair. After nearly two hours of details mingled with tears, sobs, and prolonged times of painful silence, she decided to hold a memorial service at the church to give friends and relatives an opportunity for closure. A few days later she called me and scheduled the service. It was set for August 11, 1980, at 7:00 p.m.

The service was packed with friends, relatives, and church

members, but it was grief that filled the air. I remember well maneuvering songs, Scriptures, and words of comfort around amid guttural sobs, wails, and cries of anguish. It was an incredibly sorrowful event, and it appeared to me that it ended with very little resolve for anyone in attendance.

I had no clue that this very hostile police detective, who invaded my pastoral domain for some time by then, also took an interest in—among the other victims of the Freeway Killer—this same young boy who twelve years earlier attended our church in South Gate, California.

As he described it to me that day, he didn't work directly with the case. He watched it though, with an obsessive kind of passion. His passion was not tied to a love for the mystery involved in the matter. Nor was it connected to the intrigue of finding the perpetrator. His passion was firmly anchored to an immense hostility he held in his heart for whoever could commit such an act to so many young boys.

The number of victims was in the high thirties by the time of Sean's disappearance, but before the killing spree was over, the victim count would total forty-four boys in their mid- to late-teens who were raped and murdered by the person the media—and eventually police forces—labeled as the "Freeway Killer."

In time authorities would actually discover that two killers of young boys were at work in the Los Angeles area at the same time. William George Bonin and accomplices would be indicted for fourteen murders. A second killer, whose murders were unrelated to and received less infamy than Bonin's, was dubbed the "Southern California Strangler." He was found guilty of sixteen of the forty-four murders. This left a group of fourteen murders of young men and boys, most of whom were connected to Bonin's rampage. He wasn't indicted for this group, because there wasn't enough evidence with these murders to secure a conviction. Sean was in this group, but his body wasn't even found until after Bonin was tried and convicted. It was concluded Sean's killer was Bonin, because Bonin made his home in Downey, the same city in which Sean was last seen.

This detective's disgust was also connected to the love he held for his own son. Because of this, he discovered that he hated all men who could find it within themselves to harm young boys. The repugnance he felt for whoever was responsible for these crimes was *off the charts*. He told me that when he talked about the killer, he did so with a murderous kind of disdain. At times when others at his precinct brought up the subject, his emotions would rapidly rise to rage. I had the feeling that if the killer was captured, cuffed, and sitting before him, this detective would not hesitate to put a revolver to the man's forehead and fire.

He recorded and reviewed every victim as each one was discovered. It was not his job to do so, but he couldn't leave it alone. He did extensive research on each murder and developed some of his own personal theories on who was responsible for the crimes. In addition he regularly rehearsed scenarios concerning what he would say and do to the man if he ever met him face-to-face. His diligence to put countless hours into the case was not commendable. It was more pathological. He truly hated the Freeway Killer, and it began to affect his judgment on the job and his attitude toward his work.

The disdain this detective felt for this killer and the compassion he felt for these tender lives that had been snuffed out were too much for this detective to deal with. It was during this time that a seed of disgust began to germinate in his soul for law enforcement and the animals he had to deal with every single day because of his association with it. It appeared David was in the process of making the mistake young officers are instructed emphatically not to make. He began to care.

That was twelve years before. Until the day he shared all of this information with me, he didn't know that I had a connection with the same dark story in Los Angeles history that contributed to his struggles. It would become an event that both of us would see as a binding tie, a confirmation that God brought us together.

When David finished telling his story he actually looked refreshed, but I was drained. I couldn't handle any more information that day. I made an excuse about having another appointment and gently ushered David out the door. Honestly, there was a pressing issue in my own life and David's session brought it to light.

When David left my mind went immediately to the tumultuous feelings of hatred in my own heart. I analyzed the anger I felt toward this staff person and for several minutes wrestled with those feelings. After a time I concluded that my reasons for being angry, though many would be considered justified, were not feelings I would be wise to hold on to. The potential consequences were far too great.

I also gained an added perspective from listening to David. I don't know what it was he said, but something from our session that day caused me to realize my anger wasn't just pointed at this disgruntled staff person. My anger was also aimed at God for allowing my church's attendance to yet again suffer another setback. Plain and simple, I was mad at Him for not caring about my desire to see my church grow.

Large, looming shadows of emotional darkness, which resided in my heart, became visible to me that day, and it scared me. Yes, I was angry with a former staff member, but the real anger in my soul targeted my heavenly Father. The reason it scared me so much is because it reminded me of another time in my earlier ministry days when similar feelings toward God rose in my heart.

While at my first church Shirley and I watched God do some incredible things for four years. Many people came to Christ, and the church grew by leaps and bounds. Then it stopped, and attendance began to drop off. For two years I sweated and toiled to no avail in an effort to turn the tide of decline. I was extremely stressed over it all.

Around that time my oldest son and I went on a weeklong trip. While I was on that trip I walked away from God in the privacy of my own heart. I didn't start to cuss profusely or sin defiantly. I didn't even figure I would remain away from the Lord for very long—only until our mini-vacation was over. It was just something I was going to do to show God how displeased I was that He hadn't responded to any of my prayers and efforts to make my church grow again.

I walked about thirty feet away from the Lord. I know that must sound silly, but in my mind's eye, that is exactly what I did. The next week, instead of being near to Him and He to me as it always was, I was thirty feet away from my Savior. God humored me. He must have thought about my decision and determined it would be a good lesson for me—and that it was.

I spent the next week absolutely alone. My son was there with me and had no idea concerning the foolish decision I made. But I was alone, more alone and emptier than I ever was before. Yes, even more alone than before I became a Christian. I am sure the reason I felt so abandoned was because the knowledge of being near to God was well known to me by then, having been a Christian for many years. Whereas, before I was a Christian, I had nothing to compare it to, so that week I experienced the horror of utter aloneness.

At the end of that week I closed the thirty-foot gap between God and myself, not because I concluded the lesson I was giving to God or because I felt I got my point across to Him; because neither was the case. I came back to Him, because I was tired of living in desolation. I learned that regardless of how angry I may be with God and how justified I may feel about my attitude, if it draws me away from Him even a little, it's not worth it.

So there I sat at my desk, realizing my hatred was more directed at God than it was anyone else and remembering the lesson I learned years before. I determined right then that I was going to have to release the anger I felt just for my own sanity. As I sat there I began to feel extremely sinful. As I saw it right then my anger issues went much deeper and were far more unholy than David's. I was angry with this former staff person, and I still felt as if there were a fair amount of justification for my feelings, but somehow my anger toward him was fueled by an even greater and deeper anger I felt toward God. That anger found me doing and feeling some awful things, and even worse, after considering the consequences David paid for his anger, what consequences might I end up paying if I continued to allow my anger to fester? Who was the person needing the counseling: David or myself?

CHAPTER 10

Hope Sinks

I did not see him coming or hear him enter the outer office.

It was a late afternoon in January, and it began to get dark. I contemplated whether I would stay at the church and continue working or slip back to the house so I could grab a bite to eat and then return to the church. Regardless, I was looking at very long hours on that particular day. I dozed off in my chair on purpose, thinking a few winks might do me well.

I heard him ask, "Are you busy?"

His voice startled me a little. I looked up in the direction of my office door, and there he was, peering around the doorframe. He remained in the same position until I acknowledged him.

"Not at all," I lied, uttering a silent sigh.

Detective David never came at a time that was convenient. I always seemed to be a little on my own kind of "edge" when he showed up. Each time he came, I was either behind on my sermon, pressed because of an appointment, or feeling overwhelmed because there were extra things I needed to do around the church. And yet, as I have said, I never felt the liberty to turn him away.

"Come on in," I said, motioning for him to enter.

As he came around the door I could tell he was entering my office more cautiously this day than at other times. He sat down nervously and looked away from me, around the room, and out the window.

"Are you OK?" I asked.

He wasn't limping or cringing in pain, but he looked much more tentative than ever before.

"I'm fine," he said.

"You look as if you are hurt or something," I quizzed.

"No, but I am worried about somebody." He paused for a moment and then continued, "I need to ask you for a favor," he said with noticeable hesitancy in his voice.

Each time this man came into my office, until then, David attempted to control all conversation or the lack thereof. This time, for the first time, he was relinquishing control to me.

"What is it you need?" I asked with my own degree of caution.

David launched into an explanation concerning a girl he tried to look out for on the streets. Her name was Julie. He mentioned her in an earlier session or two, but only briefly, and she hadn't come up since.

As David described it, Julie's story was not unlike any other girl's on the streets of Los Angeles. She ran away from home a few years before, but by then she was a legal adult. Tension with her parents was the factor that drove her out the door of her mid-western home when she was seventeen.

She thumbed her way to southern California, looking for a new life away from small town attitudes and what she described as "lame parents."

Out of desperation for shelter and something to eat, she wound up with the wrong crowd, on drugs, and prostituting herself to make a living.

He knew where she hung out, and he saw her most days, even if it was just to give her a smile and a head nod. He had not seen her in several days, and that concerned him. He asked a few of her friends about her that same day, and their uncertainty of her whereabouts worried him.

Several minutes went by as he filled me in on the rest of Julie's story.

"That's why I came here today," he said. "I was hoping you would go with me to find her. Maybe she's had a second overdose. I don't know if she can survive another one of those."

"When do you want to go?" I asked with obvious apprehension in my voice.

I was a bit nervous about my time and very unsure about my own safety with him alone in a car and in the hardcore city.

He hung his head, not answering for a few seconds, and then sheepishly responded as he stared at the floor, "I was hoping we could go now."

By then it was dark. I did not have anything to eat all day, but I knew I would survive, so I opted to keep my hunger to myself. I shrugged off the work I had to do, gave my wife a quick call letting her know I wouldn't be home for awhile, hopped into his car with him, and headed to who knows where.

Rush hour in Los Angeles is not the time to head for the heart of the city, but David took side streets that seemed to be exempt from the whole concept of rush hour. For an hour we snaked our way through the city streets as night fell. I saw street signs and had a general idea of which direction we were headed, but I was mostly clueless as to where we were going and where we would end up.

David didn't say a word the whole way. It was as if he weren't going to permit himself to discuss anything with me while going through the environment that made him crazy in the first place. Maybe he wanted my conversations with him to be in an "oasis setting," away from the area that made him nuts. Maybe he felt that conversation apart from my office would turn our relationship into something it wasn't supposed to be. Regardless of why, it was obvious he was uncomfortable with any discussion during this trip.

It seemed appropriate to me as well that we shouldn't talk, so I honored the silence that Detective David was intent on keeping.

I was unsure of exactly where we were when we pulled up in front of an old billiard room. I missed the street sign when we turned a few blocks back, so I didn't even know what street we were on. One hundred thirty-four was the number over the door, but the four was broken and tilted, and it looked as if there might be a number missing in front of the one.

"Well, this is it," said David. "Let's go."

We got out of the car, and I followed the nervous detective to a door on the right side of the building where the billiard room was located. We entered the front door and walked up a long, straight stairway. At the top of the stairs we entered a hallway that appeared to contain four doors, probably representing four apartments, all of which were above the billiard room we left below.

The hallway was dark and dreary with what appeared to be dingy thirty-year-old wallpaper pealing off the walls. One lone low-wattage light bulb lit the hall. The wooden floor, painted brown probably around the same time the wallpaper was hung, creaked beneath our feet. David walked to the last door in the hallway as I followed. The letter D was painted on the door in white paint. David looked at me, took a deep breath, and gently knocked on the door. I listened carefully but heard no footsteps heading for the door from the inside. David knocked again, this time a little harder...still no response. He knocked a third time and this time did so loudly.

After his third knock I could hear the faint sound of footsteps coming from one of the other apartments. I then heard the sounds of a lock unlatching, a doorknob turning, and a door squeaking open behind us. David turned and walked toward the activity. One of the doors near the head of the stairs was cracked open and a thin ray of light shone through from the crack into the hallway. A woman's face peered through the crack of the door and into the hall from beneath a chain lock.

David said, "Mrs. Jensen, is Julie home? Have you heard any noise coming from her apartment?"

The lady kept her door cracked only slightly, but responded in a rough voice that sounded as if it had been affected by throat cancer or a similar ailment.

"Haven't heard a sound for a couple of days," she said gruffly. "I figured she was on a trip."

"Could you open the door for me? I want to make sure she's all right," David said.

Apparently this lady was the caretaker who knew and trusted David, because she responded immediately, "Yeah, no problem. Just let me get my keys."

Her door closed. There was a scurry of steps, a sound consistent with a chain lock unlatching, and then Mrs. Jensen's door opened wide. A heavyset lady walked through the doorway and into the hall.

She seemed very light on her feet for someone of her size, and as she walked past us, I felt a giggle come to my face. She almost bounced as she walked. I wasn't at all familiar with deep city matters, but I would have expected a lady such as Mrs. Jensen to lumber disgustedly through her doorway, scowl at us, and then drag her depressed body down the hallway. She seemed so out of place to me.

My temptation to chuckle dissolved quickly as I looked at David; his concerned and serious demeanor kept me from it. He was noticeably worried, and that caused me to come back to earth and begin to ponder the possible scenarios we might encounter when we entered Julie's apartment.

Mrs. Jensen fumbled with her keys until she found the right one. Inserting it into the lock, she turned it and Julie's door fell open. She reached around the corner and flicked on the light. It revealed a modest but neatly kept room that contained living and kitchenette areas. David burst past me toward the one door in the room beside the entrance door. I followed close behind. He opened the door to Julie's bedroom, and there on the bed was Julie. She lay on her side with covers over her and her head on the pillow as if she were asleep, but she wasn't asleep.

David leaned over, simply touched her forehead, and stood back up again. He didn't need to check her pulse. Her cold, motionless body was all the evidence he needed. He knew she was gone. He stared at her lying on the bed for what seemed an eternity, but was really only about thirty seconds, and he seemed to have no facial expression at all for that whole time. I knew that the pain he felt as he looked at her lifeless body was enormous.

Instinctively I knew David would not careen off out of control as he was in the habit of doing in my office. These were the places he knew he had to remain in control. Ironically, his discipline to contain his emotions at times like these was likely the very thing that made him crazy.

On the stand near Julie's bed was what appeared to be an empty bottle of pills, a partially filled glass of some kind of beverage, and a note—all telltale signs of a life *resolved* to end itself.

Mrs. Jensen was still standing in the hallway. She called out, "Is Julie there? Is she OK?"

I looked at David and he looked at me as if to say, "Will you take care of that?"

I turned, walked to the hallway, and informed the bouncy, heavyset caretaker of the tragedy inside. She didn't cry.

She just said with an almost flippant tone in her voice, "Really, third one since…well, let's see…last January. Well, let me know if the detective is going to call or if he wants me to call."

With that, she spun around, bounced back down the hall into her apartment, and shut the door.

David then came out of Julie's apartment. He still had what seemed to be an emotionless expression on his face.

He said to me, "Go back to the car and stay there until this is all over. Don't get out of the car or talk to anyone. Do you understand?"

I understood perfectly. Soon other officers would be here, and David wanted to ensure that no one knew who I was or why I was there. So I obeyed like a submissive child. I went straight down the stairs, out the door, and into the car. I forgot to lock the door, so getting in wasn't a problem. I was quick to lock it once I was inside.

I began to pray. I prayed for the whole situation. I prayed for Julie's parents, whoever they might be. I prayed for the neighborhood; I prayed for Mrs. Jensen; and I prayed for David.

Within ten minutes I heard a siren drawing closer until the ambulance that produced it pulled up right behind David's car. David met the EMTs at the front door and led them upstairs to Julie's apartment. While I sat there waiting—over the next half hour—three police cars came to a stop on the street nearby. As they arrived officers exited the vehicles they came in and disappeared into the stairway leading up over the billiard room.

As I sat there I thought, *Is this going to set David back? Will it push him back over the edge again?*

David did not give me enough information about Julie to alert me to the degree of importance he placed upon his hope for a turnaround in her life…until that day. The things he shared with me just before we hopped into his car to come downtown caused me to see David wasn't just hoping, he was counting on being able to help this girl pull her life back together.

I thought, *With that hope dashed, would David be able to get his own life together?*

David stayed in Julie's apartment until the bitter end. The EMTs carried her body down the stairs on a stretcher about thirty minutes after they went up. For the next hour, one-by-one, police officers exited the downstairs door of Julie's apartment onto the street and drove off in their cars until everyone was gone. It was then that David returned to his vehicle where I sat.

He opened the driver's door, climbed in, sat down, and stared straight ahead. I saw his outbursts before, and this time I expected a bad one, but David didn't lose it.

Maybe it was because it wouldn't be appropriate for him to go psychotic outside his den of safety...*my office*. Or maybe he did not have time to process the implications of Julie's suicide as weighed against his hopes for her recovery. But that day, he held his composure.

He stared straight ahead for a minute or so before I asked him, "Are you OK?"

I wanted to reach over and embrace him, but he never granted me permission to express to him that degree of intimacy. As I asked him this question I reached over with my left hand and squeezed his right forearm in consoling fashion.

He looked back at me and didn't say a word, but his eyes seemed to say, "I don't know if I'm going to be OK or not, but I am sure glad you are here."

He placed his keys in the ignition, started the car, and we drove off. Again, silence filled the air of our trip back home. That night I had trouble sleeping, so I rolled out of bed carefully, trying not to wake my wife. I tiptoed out of our bedroom into our family room and sat down on the couch.

Our family room had a large picture window facing the street. A streetlight shone almost blaringly through the window on that part of our house at night, lighting up the whole room. If I was ever compelled to get up in the night, I made it a point to avoid this room, because the brightness there had a way of waking one up. However, this night I felt drawn to sit there.

A breeze slightly blew outside causing branches of trees to move back and forth in the wind between the streetlamp and our family room window. As I sat there that night around three in the morning, watching the shadows of trees move about in our family room, it reminded me of the frailty of man.

We are very much like branches in the wind. The breezes of life that are a great deal like the trials that come our way will toss us about in an attempt to break us. Sometimes those breezes can become destructive gales and we are helpless in our efforts to shore ourselves up at those times. Whatever growth or strength we have acquired prior to those winds randomly blowing against us will be all the strength we will have available to us. So we better have enough, or we will be broken and thrust to the ground.

As I pondered this, for the first time I began to feel great compassion for my odd counselee. Did David have enough strength to weather this breeze…this wind…this gale? I began to weep for him and pray that God would grant him the strength to withstand the storms in his life that were bent on breaking him.

I listened to an incredible amount of information from this troubled lawman, and I was moved many times, but that night Detective David got into my heart.

CHAPTER 11

Distractions

People who know me well are aware that I am very easily distracted.

When I study I close all the windows and shades so that sights and sounds don't deter me. Some, especially my wife, have wondered how creative I could possibly be because of the boxlike environment I prefer to work in when I compile my writings and sermons. For me to try to prepare a message while sitting on a rock on the side of a mountain would be an exercise in futility. If a miracle occurred and I ever did complete a sermon out in nature, it would probably result in a powerless presentation the following Sunday. The birds singing, the squirrels chattering, the bees buzzing, and the breezes blowing would completely occupy my mind while saying nothing to me along spiritual lines.

While in my office, if I am fortunate enough to have a creative thought and I am interrupted, you may as well kiss that thought good-bye.

While presenting sermons or teaching a class, if a baby happens to be present and begins to cry and scream or just *goo* and *gaa*, I may never recapture my thought or find my place in my notes again.

Reading is no different. High concentration is an illusive mental ability for me. Noise, movement, smells, and tastes are surefire deterrents to my gathering quality information from any book or article. I could never eat a bowl of cherry ice cream while reading a story and hope to understand or remember anything I've read.

On a larger scale, I am very goal-oriented and distractions on the way to reaching my goals are significantly disruptive to me. This trait drives my wife crazy on trips. She would like to stop and smell the roses. I would like to get where we are going. Smelling roses, seeing sights, skipping stones, eating dinner, going to the bathroom, and a host of other meaningless activities are all distractions from the most important task on any trip—reaching our destination. When lost, asking directions is the first thing I do, not the last. My primary goal is to get to my destination, not to prove that I can find my way.

On a more spiritual note, it is peculiar to me why God called me into pastoral ministry since it requires numerous weekly deadlines. The ministry of a pastor by its very nature requires distractions. It is part of the job description. Emergencies, hardships, crises, problems, and difficulties can fall into your lap in a moment's notice, and you better be ready. It does not matter that you have a sermon that must be prepared weekly like clockwork, sometimes more than one. A pastor's job is to have your pre-determined pastoral work (such as sermons) ready on time and to handle all the crises that come up, regardless of whether or not time allows. That part of the job never seemed to be a fit for me, because distractions always seem to attempt to prohibit me from meeting my deadlines.

This propensity I have toward being goal-oriented has also played itself out in the objectives I set early on in my ministry. As you've already read, I set my sights on *glory* (*thirty-eight seconds* worth), characterized by increasing numbers when I was just a young man. For most of my life I have pursued that objective, refusing to be distracted by any competing activities, opinions, or philosophies.

Detective David was more than a distraction from the task-oriented deadlines I was bound to each week. He was a distraction from the objectives I set for my whole life. I set goals of success, renown, numbers, and *glory*, and each time he came to my door, what he represented stood symbolically as an obstacle smack-dab in the middle of my road to reach my goals. This was made clear to me one disappointing day.

I received a call from the office of a renowned spiritual leader who was going to be in my area. Because I showed support for his ministry, he invited me, along with about fifteen other pastors who supported him, to a brunch on a specific day. The purpose was to meet him, dialogue about ministry, and form relationships.

I was so excited I couldn't sleep the night before. I woke up early that morning and showered, rushed through my devotions, and went to the church to work on things so I could free myself up for the brunch that day. I studied for a few hours, packed up my briefcase, and tidied my desk. As I was about to leave, I bent over in my chair to tie my shoe and then stood turning to the door to leave. When I did, there stood David.

His presence in my doorway was such a shock to me it scared me. I actually uttered a gasp and jumped back. I said, "David, you scared me." He didn't say a word. When I settled myself and focused my eyes on him, I was able to look closer. As I did, I could see that he wasn't right. His hair was completely disheveled. His face was dirty and tear-stained. He wore a suit coat and tie, but the coat was soiled and the necktie though tied was draped loosely around his neck. The top two buttons of his shirt were unbuttoned, not by human choice, but by what appeared to be force, because the button holes were torn and his white shirt was ripped and possessed what looked like a grass stain on its front.

I said, "David, are you all right?" It was a stupid question though, because I could see he wasn't.

Then I realized the dilemma I was in. I had a brunch I was scheduled to attend in my sights. It wasn't just any old brunch. This was the type of meeting I waited for my whole life.

I was never fortunate enough to be personally mentored by a pastor or church leader, but I unofficially chose the pastor holding the brunch that day as my "mentor from a distance." I began to read all his books and listen to his tapes in an effort to shape my ministry around his. Now I had an opportunity to sit with him across a breakfast table, meet him personally, and absorb his wisdom. I saw it as a chance of a lifetime.

I also had what appeared to be a desperate need standing before me. I didn't want to spend two hours with David that day. I had what I felt were *more important fish to fry*.

I stood there looking at him with my mouth open but silent for several seconds, waiting for him to say something, and honestly, I didn't know what to say.

Finally David spoke. With his voice quivering, he said, "I've got to talk with you. I...I...don't know what to do."

I was still speechless, but I was screaming inside. I felt angry; I felt put out; I felt used; I felt as if I had an anchor by the name of David hanging around my neck. I wanted to grit my teeth and sneer at him in hateful disgust, but he was looking straight into my eyes. I knew at that moment, by the vulnerability I detected on his face, any truth-revealing facial expression from me would not be appropriate.

Finally I managed, "Well...I..." I was trying to tell him I had an important appointment I was supposed to attend, and I was on my way out the door, but I couldn't make myself finish the sentence. I was in the middle of one of the fiercest battles of my ministry, and I was fighting it right there in front of David.

He didn't let me stand there for long. He finally said, "Steve's wife committed suicide."

My heart sank. I knew David needed me more than ever right then, and I began to feel the brunch slipping away.

I said somewhat sympathetically, "David, I'm so sorry. Sit down." I glanced at my briefcase on the floor beside my desk as David sat down in one of my guest chairs. Then I sat down in the other.

I looked at David. His head was down, and he was sniffling slightly. His legs were separated and he was bent over with his elbows resting on his knees. His hands were clasped together as he stared at the floor. It had been a while since

David's last visit with me. I lost track of just how long it was since we last went into the city together. That time had also been laden with bad news—bad news that was similar to the news that day.

I was truly conflicted as I watched him sitting in my office that morning. I thought, *Do I get to have a life of my own? Can I ever be free to do what I want?* Here David was again, disrupting my schedule. I felt somewhat sorry for him, but I also felt a bit sorry for myself and quite angry with him for inconveniencing me yet again. I didn't want to be pampering a hopeless crazy person. I wanted to be with my successful hero at the brunch. It was probably my only chance to connect with him and here I was stuck with David.

As I sat there I grew angrier by the minute. I started to analyze the irony of the situation. I wanted to have a big successful ministry, and the man at the brunch had a proven track record in that area. I hoped to glean some of that big-ministry wisdom from him; maybe even make a connection that might begin an ongoing relationship with him that could expose me to his ministry savvy on a more regular basis.

And here I was, saddled with a man for whom I felt little hope; and I was 100 percent convinced he would never contribute to the *increase* of my church. Furthermore, he drained time and energy from me that I could devote to more productive exploits.

Finally I said to him in a tone that was reflective of the frustration I felt, "What happened, David?" I noticed the anger in my words to him, but I didn't care. I continued deliberately, "How did you find this out?"

David apparently didn't notice the coldness in my voice,

because he kept his head down staring at the floor in the same position he was in when he first sat down. It seemed if he noticed he would have looked up to see if I was upset, but he didn't.

With his head still down he said, "When I got to work early this morning, the captain pulled me into his office and told me. Apparently she just received word that her and Steve's daughter was autistic. I guess she couldn't deal with the stress of raising a troubled kid by herself. She made arrangements for her daughter and then brought her to her sister's house. Then she went into her garage, turned on the car, and went to sleep. She was there all afternoon. She had been dead two hours yesterday before they found her."

My sympathetic side had yet to kick in. I was still entertaining hope that I might be able to cut the counseling short so I could make at least some of my appointment. So I went into my "quick-fix mode," hoping I could pacify his pain and usher him out of my office so I could be on my way.

I said, "You know, David. There is no reason why you should think that what she did to herself was your fault. People commit suicide every day for reasons that have little to do with good judgment. They're just depressed…irrational. They just don't…"

David cut me off. He looked up at me and said abruptly, "She put my name in her suicide note. She blamed me for Steve's death."

That information didn't sidetrack me, either. I was still in fix-it mode and said, "But how could she blame you, David? Accidents just happen."

Again David interrupted me and said, "Please, just listen."
David collected himself and began to talk. "When they
first made Steve my partner, Susan and I had him and his
wife over to the house for a barbeque. While sitting around
the dinner table, she stopped the conversation, quieted
everyone, and said..."

David stopped at this point and took a deep breath. I saw
his eyes begin to tear up. It was clear that he was mustering
courage for his next words.

David went on, "She said to me, 'David, I want you
to promise me that you won't let anything happen to my
husband. Do you promise?' I remember it as if it were
yesterday. I just said, 'I promise. I promise' like it was no big
deal."

The tears from David's eyes were flowing freely now, and
his voice was quivering and desperate.

He went on, "Then she said, 'No, David. I mean it. Do you
promise?' That's when I looked at her in the eye and said,
'I promise. Nothing will happen to Steve as long as he's my
partner.'"

When David said this I came back to reality concerning
my brunch. I still wasn't pleased with the interruption,
but I knew then that I wasn't going to be able to make my
appointment. So I settled in for the duration, but I wasn't
happy about it.

I then asked David, "What did the note say?" in a bit
more sympathetic tone than I used with my last series of
questions.

He responded sheepishly, "It said, 'David promised me he
would keep Steve safe. I should never have trusted him.'"

Then David looked at me and said, "She's right. It's my fault. I know it is. I felt Steve was too relaxed and I should have said something, but I didn't. Now I'm responsible for two people being dead."

I didn't know what to say to him, so I changed the subject. "David, why is your coat dirty and your shirt ripped?" I asked.

My first thought was that maybe he had been in some kind of scuffle with a suspect he encountered, but quickly dismissed that option. Then I wondered if perhaps he reverted back to some of his self-destructive behavior over the suicide incident we were discussing.

He took a few moments to collect himself before he answered. Then he said, "The captain gave me the rest of the day off, so I went to this place I go to sometimes. It's a little park up in the foothills. I did a stakeout there once for a drug deal. No one ever goes there, so I stop by there sometimes to think. It's peaceful."

He stopped as if he finished what he was saying. I wasn't in quick-fix mode anymore, but I was still frustrated enough to be short and abrupt with him.

I said, "But that doesn't answer my question. What did you do to your coat and shirt? You seem to be trying to avoid my question."

David looked at me a little funny, as if he were confused by my brashness. David wasn't at all overly sensitive. As brazen as he was in his communication with me from the time he first stepped into my office a few years back, it was apparent he had some thick skin himself. My guess was that he was used to some straight and no-nonsense talk. But he hadn't heard me be that direct, and his look reflected surprise that I was being so deliberate with him.

He responded, "Well, if you must know, I was tempted to hurt myself, but I decided I'd try hurting my clothes instead."

I looked at him somewhat surprised, and he looked at me, waiting to see what my reaction was going to be. Then all at once, a smile began to form on both our faces, and we held our grins for several moments.

Finally I said, "David, everyone is looking for someone to blame. Just because Steve's wife blamed you doesn't mean it's your fault."

David responded, "Yeah, that's what the captain said. It doesn't console me though. Two people are dead, and I feel like there must have been something I could have done. But whatever it was I didn't think of it, so I didn't do it. In my book that means I have to accept some of the blame."

I looked at David with a little impatience and a little suspicion. It felt a bit like he was playing a popular mind game with me. You know the game. It's called *The Yes-But Game*. It's the game where nothing you suggest will ever help, not in this life or the next one, because he doesn't want it to. In this game David decided to be at fault, and nothing was going to change his mind. It's really a self-pity game. I seldom have time to play that game, but this day especially, my patience for this kind of thing was quite low.

Assuming this was what David was doing, I sighed and said even more deliberately than before, "Listen, David. A drug dealer killed your partner, Steve, not you. He used a gun and a bullet. You didn't turn your gun on Steve. And

Steve's wife killed herself. You didn't kill her. She used her car's exhaust. You didn't turn the car on or close all the windows. You can feel bad because your guesswork wasn't accurate that day, but you didn't possess the intentionality that the drug dealer possessed, and you didn't decide to kill Steve's wife. She made that decision all by herself. You didn't kill anyone."

I surprised myself with my candor, and it was apparent that David was taken aback by it as well. But deep in my heart I knew what was going on. I felt sorry for David and his new dilemma and he probably was playing a little game with me, but I was still feeling put out over David's intrusion into my plans that day. So I was in "no-nonsense mode" even though I knew that the brunch with my ministry hero was a lost opportunity.

By then David knew he wasn't going to receive great amounts of sympathy from me. It seemed that was OK, because after David got over the shock of my boldness, he responded, "You know what? You're probably right. I guess I was feeling sorry for myself a little...or maybe a lot. It looks like I ruined a good shirt for nothing."

We talked a little more about the tragedy of that day, and then I prayed with David and sent him on his way. I stood at the front office door, watching David walk to his car. Then I turned and stepped back into my office. On my desk was a note I wrote out and was going to tape to the outside door. It read, "SORRY, OUT FOR BRUNCH. I'LL BE BACK THIS AFTERNOON. CHRIS." I crumpled it up, threw it in the wastebasket, sat down, and began to move reluctantly back into my work.

THE MAIN THING

Have you heard this statement before? "Keep the main thing the main thing."

I have learned over the years that certain things we perceive to be important can become distractions to us. This was true of the brazen serpent in Numbers. It was originally made to be the focal point for healing from God as people would focus their gaze upon it. Yet, generations later, it actually became a distraction to the people's worship of God. Similarly, certain problem issues, while it is important to deal with them as they arise, can become major distractions that sidetrack us from focusing on what is truly important.

For example, I have found myself zeroing in on trying to fix a critical attitude emerging in my church, while leaving important ministry issues unattended. I did this because I perceived that the critical attitude was distracting our church from its main objectives of love and unity. Therefore, it was a key issue that needed to be dealt with, so I dealt with the attitude. Soon I would find the issue rising up again in someone else. Then it would start to affect others, so I would talk about it with related parties. Then I would feel I should talk to church leadership about it because it became a more grave concern. Then I would feel I needed to address it in a Sunday sermon. Then someone would misinterpret what I was saying, so I would have to explain myself. Before long I found I was fairly consumed with what I thought was an important issue to start with, but ultimately became something that was more of a diversion from what was important. In the end the issue became a significant distraction that I wasn't sure how to reverse. I became stuck in "distraction mode."

Jesus possessed an uncanny ability to detect what was *the main thing* and what were distractions from *the main thing*.

According to Matthew 16, one day Jesus was instructing His disciples about *the main thing*. He asked them who people thought He was. His disciples were into the teaching and one of them, Peter, made the declaration that Jesus was the Messiah, the Son of God. Then Jesus moved from there into telling them how powerful the church will be against hell's gates as it carries the message of His Messiahship (Peter's discovery) to the world. Then He began to talk to them about how it was all going to come down in His death and resurrection. He talked about *the main thing*. Nothing in all of God's Word was more important than what Jesus talked about that day.

Suddenly the same Peter who was so right-on only minutes earlier became a distraction. He said, "No way, Lord. I won't let anyone kill You" (Matt. 16:22, author's paraphrase).

Peter thought he was being noble, supportive, sensitive, and loyal. I am relatively sure that if I had been standing beside him, I would have offered him a high five and given him a cheer for his sensitivity to the Savior.

Jesus detected the distraction. He said, "Get behind Me, Satan! You are an offense to Me, for you are not mindful of the things of God, but the things of men" (Matt. 16:23).

Another time when Jesus was teaching His disciples, parents brought their children to be blessed by Him. The disciples considered these visitors to be a distraction from *the main thing*. They tried to shoo the parents and their little ones away. When Jesus saw what was going on, He rebuked

His disciples and said, "Let the little children to come to Me, and do not forbid them; for such is the kingdom of God" (Mark 10:14).

His disciples thought the kids were a distraction from *the main thing*. Jesus saw that the children were *the main thing*.

Some time after David altered my brunch plans, I realized that he wasn't a distraction from *the main thing*. He was *the main thing*, sent to bring me back from what distracted me my entire life. My zeal early on was good. My desire to do my best for the Master was a righteous mind-set. Somewhere along the way I became distracted from what the ministry was all about—people.

It wasn't that the man holding the brunch was a bad or wrong influence on me—not at all. He was and still is a great man who God has used mightily. It was that, in my heart, I saw him as another means by which I might be able to chase down my illusive dream of success and prominence in the ministry. In short, because of the way *I* perceived things at the time, this dear pastor became the distraction in my life—a distraction from *the main thing*, people.

At that time, as I played out the part of the disciples, I saw David as the distraction.

Interestingly, I never received a call from this leader to come to other gatherings, brunches, lunches, or otherwise. I sent my regrets explaining what happened. I don't know if he had similar events but chose not to invite me, or decided to abandon the idea of having these kinds of meetings with pastors altogether. But it seems I forfeited my opportunity for that kind of interaction forever. I'm OK with it, though. I would rather be certain that I am focused on *the main thing*.

CHAPTER 12

The Shake-Up

On a Sunday night in January of 1994, our whole family stayed up to watch a movie. We hit the sack around two in the morning and fell instantly asleep. Martin Luther King's birthday was the next day. It was a holiday, and we could all sleep in.

It seemed as if my eyes had been closed only a few seconds when I was jolted out of my slumber and to my feet. For a split second, it seemed as if someone like David had startled me as he had a way of doing. But very quickly it was apparent that this startling experience had nothing to do with David.

As I stood by my bed our whole house was being jerked about viciously. It took only moments for me to realize we were well into the most violent earthquake any of us ever encountered.

I lived in California for seventeen years and our family experienced many minor quakes. I called them adrenaline teasers. They summoned minor secretions of adrenaline that actually made them appear to be fun.

I even thought at different times, *What's the big deal about earthquakes?*

However, on January 17, 1994 at 4:31 a.m., my opinions about earthquakes changed forever.

As I stood beside my bed, the earth convulsed and the house around us threatened to collapse. I was surrounded by what seemed to be the noise of a freight train within just a few feet of my head. At that moment better sense captured me, so I gingerly felt for the bed behind me and sat carefully down upon it. Yet the bed, along with our house and everything in it, continued to shake angrily.

By this time my wife was on her knees on top of the mattress. She pushed me and said with a frantic pitch to her voice, "Chris, go get the kids. Please, go get Jeff and Joel."

Our bedroom was on one end of our ranch-style house. Both of our sons, one in junior high and the other college age, were in their bedrooms at the complete other end of our home.

In response to her panicked request I stood up, preparing to go and rescue our two boys. I took one step away from the bed and was struck by something on my forehead. It knocked me to the floor. I wasn't dazed, but the blow tempered my boldness to hurry after our sons. I stood up from the floor and began my journey toward the other end of the house a second time, but this time more cautiously. Shirley followed close behind, hanging on to my pajamas.

The earthquake eliminated all of the electricity. I reached for the light switch and clicked it up and down several times with no response. For some reason I felt sweat trickling from my brow into my eyes. So I wiped my forehead periodically as I felt my way through the darkness toward our children's bedrooms.

Glass from picture frames, light bulbs, and vases was lying broken on the floor. I couldn't see any of it in the dark, but I felt it beneath me. It was a miracle that my bare feet weren't slashed and bleeding.

As I made my way through our house, still unable to see in the dark, I tripped over a chair in my path, chipping a bone in my right foot. All the while, the earthquake continued to vibrate furiously, seemingly shaking our house to its collapsible limits. I felt that it should break apart and crumble to the ground at any moment.

They tell you not to move in an earthquake for all the reasons I just mentioned. I should have stayed put on my bed, but parental responsibility prevailed and was largely responsible for the injuries I sustained. Come to find out, the sweat trickling from my forehead was blood from whatever hit me on my head in the bedroom. As I wiped it from my brow and felt my way through the house in the dark, I left a blood trail behind me on the walls. The next day I waited in a two-hour-long line at a nearby hospital, along with others who were also injured in the earthquake, to have my forehead stitched back up.

After making my way through about two-thirds of the house, I stopped to yell to my older son, "Jeff, are you OK?"

He yelled back, "Dad…this…is…the…big…one!"

One of the most common discussions over coffee in southern California is the imminent danger of the big earthquake that seismologists predicted for decades, commonly called, "The Big One."

Ignoring what I thought to be the obvious, I screamed back, "Are you in the doorway?"

"Yes!" He shouted back.

"Get your brother and stay under the doorframe," I told him.

I then turned and felt my way to the kitchen to find the flashlight. All the while, Shirley was close behind me. When I entered the kitchen I was taken aback by the amount of debris I felt under my feet. I couldn't identify it by touch, but something told me most of it represented broken glass. I knew, however, though my feet weren't protected by shoes, that concern could not stop me. I needed to press on.

I came to the cupboard where the flashlight was located and reached up for it. The door was wide open and completely devoid of its contents. Instantly, I knew the quake cleared the cupboard entirely and what was inside could only have fallen onto the floor. Instinctively I went to my knees and began to feel for the flashlight through the clutter on the floor around me. Surprisingly I found it rather quickly and switched it on immediately. As I shined it frantically around the kitchen, I was awed by what I saw.

Every cupboard was open and empty. Every plate, bowl, cup, piece of glassware, and china was either smashed on our tile counter or in pieces on the floor. Every small appliance, pan, pitcher, candle, knick-knack, spice, can, jar of food, or other miscellaneous item that happened to be stored in our kitchen cupboards, was thrust to the floor as well. The floor of our kitchen was two inches deep in shattered glassware and debris. I saw all that in a brief moment.

Our house was still shaking, so I turned the flashlight toward the floor in front of me and headed in the direction of the front entrance. I shouted for our boys to leave the doorway they were standing under and meet us there. By the time we all reached our front door, the initial jolts of the quake subsided and we all scurried outside together.

It wasn't any easier to see standing in front of our house. It was as pitch black outside as it was inside because all of the streetlights, along with every house light inside and out, was extinguished by the blackout from the quake.

The most frightening moments of the earthquake, however, took place in the first few seconds after we came to a halt together on the sidewalk in front of our home. We saw and heard explosions coming from every direction. We surmised that the sources of these explosions were transformers that were hanging on electrical poles all around the area.

Some huge explosions could be heard and seen to our west and were accompanied by enormous flashes of light. We later learned that they were from the science lab at California State University at Northridge (CSUN). The whole lab was lost.

Amid these explosions were the sounds of people screaming and crying for help coming from inside the houses around us. Windows were broken by the quake, revealing the frantic cries of those who were still trapped inside houses.

One lady from across the street called out, "Help me, please! I'm trapped!"

A man responded loud enough for us to hear, "I'm coming. Move away from the door."

We could hear the whimpering of both children and adults coming from two or three different directions. We also heard near and distant voices coming from all around the neighborhood, probing for responses from family members in attempts to find out their status.

Then there was the sound of running water. It became clear that large amounts of water were flowing down the street in front of our house. At first I thought it was from water pipes that broke, which alarmed me greatly. Later we learned that the water was from swimming pools. The earthquake shook so violently that it caused huge quantities of water to slosh over the sides of the many pools in our neighborhood. Water poured down driveways of homes all around the neighborhood and into the streets. We were downhill so the water came our way. Yet for several minutes, this sound of water rushing down our street concerned us.

The initial jolts of the quake lasted about forty seconds, but it was followed within minutes by many aftershocks, some nearly as strong as the original quake. As we stood outside our home we could hear sirens and alarms coming from everywhere. All the while, we could feel the constant shaking under our feet. We truly felt as if we were experiencing the end of the world. As we stood there in the dark, we were absolutely gripped by fear. We huddled together in an attempt to ward off the terror that surrounded us.

Though I didn't voice it at the time, there was a prevailing concern deep in my heart. It was a weight on my mind. It was so dark I couldn't see, but in the back of my thoughts was the nagging fear that our church was lying flat on the ground like the leveled walls of Jericho. The church was located about one hundred fifty yards to our west at the front of the church property. In the daylight and even at night in the city lights, its outline dominates the western skyline as viewed from our house. But there were no lights, and the pitch-blackness hid the building's condition from our sight.

In addition to the possible annihilation of our church structure was an underlying fear that my congregation may also be in the throes of disintegration. How many may die? How many may be displaced? I had no idea what the earthquake may do to the fibers of my future. As I stood there, it was a splinter piercing my mind. My ministry success issues, it seems, were still prone to rushing to the forefront of my consciousness, even amid great crisis. I knew no one would understand if I voiced them. So I spoke nary a word of my concerns while we were gathered there in the darkness on the front sidewalk of our home.

My mind was yanked back to reality by the sight of a strange orange glow in the sky to our north that had the makings of an enormous fire. My younger son strained his neck in the excitement, and, as a result, wasn't game for much movement. So my older son and I hurried up the driveway toward the front of the church to see if we could learn the origin of the glow. I was greatly relieved as I passed our church building on the way to the street to see that it was still standing. Our church sat on Balboa Boulevard, one of the main arteries in the San Fernando Valley. The street ran straight as an arrow from the north to the south. We desired to peer up the boulevard, hoping to learn where this glow was coming from.

Sure enough, about a mile up the street, somewhere in the neighborhood of Balboa Boulevard's intersection with the Simi Valley Freeway, enormous flames were shooting out from what appeared to be the street itself. We found out later that day that a gas main broke in the middle of Balboa Boulevard, caught fire, and was sending flames high into the air. To complicate matters, a water main adjacent to the gas main broke as well and the gushing water carried the burning gas down driveways into nearby properties, catching homes on fire. Several houses at that location burned to the ground. We gazed at the fire for only a short while, because I felt the need to return to the house where my wife and younger son were still standing.

Meanwhile, we all felt very uneasy about going back into the house in the dark while the ground was still shaking. So I backed our car out of the garage, parked it several feet away from any structures, turned the heat on, and we sat inside to keep warm. But just the same, darkness and terror were all around us.

There were a couple of single ladies in our church who roomed together nearby. We decided to risk driving to their home to make sure they were all right.

As we drove through the streets we could sense the terror all around. Almost no one was outside that we could see, yet it was hard to tell, because it was pitch black both in and outside every house we passed. The only lights visible were our own headlights. We had the feeling that people were sitting in their houses, wide awake and paralyzed with fear. Our concern escalated as we drove cautiously through the streets.

When we arrived at their house both ladies were sitting on the curb in front of their home in their pajamas. One of the ladies had a son, and he was huddled between the two ladies trying to feel safe. We took a few moments to converse with them and become assured that they were secure, and then we turned around and headed back to our own home. Arriving, we waited there in our car until it was light before we went back into our house again.

Upon entering our home we were aghast. It looked like a battle zone. Bookcases fell and books were strewn all over the floor in every room. Knick-knacks, pictures, plants, and lamps were scattered everywhere. It seemed as if everything that could have broken was broken. My wife's twenty-five piece Precious Moments collection and a very expensive Lladro porcelain figurine were in pieces and scattered all over the living room floor. Two television sets tipped over and both picture tubes were cracked. Furniture fell over and broke. Almost every breakable dish in the kitchen was shattered.

We did not do a precise inventory of the destroyed items in our house, but rough "guesstimates" tallied between four and five thousand dollars worth of personal items lost and worthy of being trashed.

I saw shows where people were interviewed after disasters such as tornadoes and hurricanes. Those questioned made statements to the effect that they weren't sorrowful over the loss of their possessions. They were just thankful to have escaped with their lives. I remembered watching them and thinking that their answers sounded a bit theatrical, perhaps even staged. But when the Northridge Earthquake hit, all of my perceptions about these kinds of things changed. I suddenly felt sympathy for any and all people ravaged by disasters. I felt absolutely no sadness over losing thousands of dollars worth of valuables. We were just happy to be alive.

Only one of my wife's Precious Moments pieces was spared from breaking, and it was the piece that appeared to have been traumatized the most. In the earthquake it became wedged between our piano and the wall. As you know, a piano is very heavy. As the quake jerked and convulsed, it yanked our piano around as well. While the shaking was going on, the piano trapped the porcelain piece against the wall and forced it violently through the drywall behind the instrument. When the dust settled there was a neatly formed hole in our wall behind the piano the exact size of the head of the clay piece. The figure was lying on the floor seemingly unaffected. It was the only piece of the collection that suffered no damage. It seemed to represent the mystery of God's power to protect the most fragile of lives—even amid such great destruction.

For the next few hours we tried to bring a semblance of order to our home. All the while, aftershocks continued every few minutes, each one sending yet another adrenaline rush throughout my body.

Later, when I felt my family was safe, I went back to the front of the property to inspect inside and outside the church. To my relief and surprise, damage was minimal. Many churches around the area were not so fortunate. Scores of church buildings were condemned by earthquake inspection teams. Ours was not.

Surprisingly, within a few hours our phones began to work. About the time we heard a dial tone the phone rang and kept on ringing. Family, friends, and church members were calling to check on us and to let us know their status. Within an hour after the earthquake our families on the other side of the country heard about the disaster that took place in our city. Pictures were being displayed all over the airwaves of buildings that collapsed within only a few blocks of our home. But, of course, with our electricity out we couldn't see any of it.

One single mom in our church by the name of Christine called us about midway through the first day to let us know that her apartment building was so extensively damaged that her managers spread word around the complex that they would be asking everyone to leave and they would prohibit people from coming back into the building. It was too dangerous. She called us to ask if there was anyone who could help her move her belongings out of her apartment that afternoon.

My oldest son and I were the only ones available to help her. Actually we had plenty to do just reorganizing our own home, but her situation seemed a bit more crucial. She had a friend who owned a truck she could use, but no one was free to offer her any assistance. So we put on our moving hats.

When we pulled up to her apartment, we gazed in disbelief. It looked as if bombs fell and exploded all around her building. An entire outside wall fell flat to the ground, revealing the insides of all the apartments on that side of the building.

As we stood looking in awe she said to us, "Do you see the third one from the end on the second floor with the black couch? That's my apartment."

As I stared in wonder I was struck with the awareness that many people in our church lived in apartments just like the one I was looking at. Again the thought came to me, *How many people are we going to lose through this?* It was a momentary and perhaps self-absorbed thought, but it was there nonetheless.

To get to the second floor we had to enter the building on one end and climb the stairs to Christine's floor. It was a scary endeavor. The stairway was separated away from the wall about two feet, and the stairs swayed as we went up.

Her apartment was as cluttered as our house. She had a good idea about what items were the most vital for us to take and what was expendable. We moved as quickly as possible for two obvious reasons. First, so we could get as many of her personal belongings out of the apartment as we could before we were asked to leave for good. The word was, once the buildings were closed down, all the contents would be condemned with the structures.

The second reason we needed to work quickly was for our own safety. It seemed as if only a slight nudge would cause the whole building to collapse completely, and aftershocks were occurring regularly. Our nerves were frayed as we moved all this lady had left of her life down the stairs and into the truck.

To make the situation even more unnerving, as we were carrying items down the stairs, other tenants were doing the same thing. The floating staircase was a thoroughfare of people desperately trying to retrieve as many of their belongings as they could before it was too late. It seemed miraculous to me that we were able to complete the job without the stairs or any more walls collapsing.

We worked quickly and with focus on the task at hand, but in my mind I entertained thoughts that weren't very noble. I thought, *Am I actually helping this lady move away?*

Our church is diminishing before my eyes and at my hands, and I am willingly helping it to do so. Furthermore, I am risking my own life to help make it happen.

Then I aimed my not-so-wholesome thinking heavenward. I wondered, *God, what are You doing to me? Not only are You taking people from me, You are demanding that I help You do it.*

I couldn't believe the irony of it all. Something in me wanted to drop what I was toting and childishly say to Christine, "If you have to leave our church through all this, get someone else to help you." About halfway down the floating staircase on one of my trips, as if God sent it to cleanse my soiled thoughts, an aftershock jolted my mind out of the gutter and back to what I was doing.

It took us less than an hour to salvage her necessary belongings. We then hopped in the truck and drove her to the house where she arranged to store her goods. We had to drive by way of backstreets though, because the freeways to the storage location were severely damaged by the earthquake, and roadblocks were set up, refusing us passage. After we unloaded, Christine had no place to stay, so we invited her to spend the night with us.

When the three of us finally arrived home, it was almost dark. As I walked through the door my wife informed me that all of the college students who attended our church and who lived in the dorms were rendered homeless by the earthquake, and six of them needed a place to stay for the night. We let them camp out on the floor of our home along with Christine. There were eleven of us who spent the night at our house that next evening after the quake.

Now remember, our family only managed to get about two

and a half hours of sleep the night before the earthquake, so we were extremely tired. The next night was not at all kind to us as far as sleep was concerned, because the aftershocks kept coming. If we were fortunate enough to fall asleep in between *the all too frequent* jolts, as soon as the next one hit, we would all wake up again. The ugly truth was that they kept us so uneasy while we waited for the next one to come that it was nearly impossible to sleep at all. To complicate the sleep issue my wife insisted that our whole family sleep in the same bed for her peace of mind. We only had a queen-sized mattress, so the four of us slept sideways in our bed. Believe me, this arrangement did not lend itself to increasing the amount of sleep we might receive that night. I don't know how much slumber we managed that next night, but it had to have been even less than we received the night before.

In the morning all of our guests found places to go where they could be more comfortable and better cared for. As we said good-bye to them we had the sense that we would never see them again, and such was the case.

It took us three full days to get our heat, electricity, and water back. It was nearly a week before I was able to get a respectable amount of sleep.

What a shake-up! Not just for my family and our church, I was shaken up personally. I felt adrenaline rushes for two years afterward because of the earthquake. Every time someone would mildly bump a chair I sat in, butterflies would dance furiously within me. That wasn't the shake-up that had me the most unsettled.

It was as if God were shaking the foundation of my values to the very core. Looking back, I have to admit they needed a shake-up. Every time our church saw any kind of a surge in growth, my satisfaction level would rise. Then some incident out of my control would bring it tumbling down again. Now it was the earthquake. It attacked some of my most prized values with violent fury.

The quake shook up our church as well, and as it shook, it sifted. My worst fears concerning our fellowship while the ordeal was going on were realized. The twenty-five students from CSUN, who called our church their home, were all rendered homeless when state inspection teams condemned their dorms. Each moved back into their parents' homes, all of which lived in other parts of the state or country. We lost them all. In addition, approximately fifteen others in our church, including Christine, lived in apartment buildings that were condemned, and like our college students, had to move in with relatives out of the area. The Northridge earthquake ran forty people out of our church.

This infamous event in southern California history shook the foundations of my life and ministry. As I received call after call from people informing me that they had to move away and wouldn't be attending my church anymore, I found myself not just asking, but screaming the same question I asked while moving Christine's things. "God…why? Why are You allowing this to happen to me?"

What I didn't recognize at the time was that in my very question was my answer. Somewhere along the way I formed the idea that the growth of my church was about me. If God should cause my church to grow, I thought it was for my benefit, my needs, my ego, my success, my acclaim, and my future.

But the growth of my church was never about me; not when I first entered the ministry; not when my ministry experienced *much* growth; and not when it experienced *little* growth. It was always about Him, His church, His name, His glory, and His purposes.

It took a compassionate and sovereign God to shake up the supporting beams of my life so I could begin to see the flaws in my thinking and the errors in my heart.

I still feel a little shaken up and wonder what it will ultimately mean for me in the long run. I seem to have gotten over the adrenaline rushes that used to occur when I was nudged by accident while sitting on chairs and couches, but I am not sure I will ever get over the shake-up *God* brought to my life. I am not sure I want to. Though it was traumatizing while it happened, it has turned out to be a defining shake-up in my life—a truly divine *rattling of my proverbial cage*.

CHAPTER 13

Perspectives

One day, a few weeks after the earthquake, I looked out of my office window in time to see David's car pull up. I stopped what I was doing and with interest watched him get out of his car and begin his familiar saunter to my office. As I observed him draw nearer to my front door, I suddenly realized I wasn't dreading his coming. That was a remarkable turnaround in thinking, considering my frustration concerning the timing of his last visit. Instead I felt as if it were going to be good to see him. Something inside me felt an incredible sense of compassion for him. Oddly, considering the way I used to feel when he came by, that day I felt like a comrade was about to drop by to express his friendship.

As he came through my office door, I rose to greet him, stepped toward him, and embraced him. He hugged me back and began to cry. His crying quickly turned into light sobs and shook us both as we stood there embracing. Tears came to my eyes as well.

Within a few moments he collected himself, disentangled from the embrace, and sat down. I sat in the other guest chair. As I did, I realized it had been a long time since

I used my desk as a barrier between us for my safety. I smiled inwardly as I thought about this.

It was only a few moments before he began to form words, but a flood of memories rushed into my head as I waited. I recalled his first visit with the shouting and pacing. I remembered the day of silence and the time I asked him if my life was in danger because I learned his name. I wanted to grin again, but I knew he was looking at me, so I kept my face from forming a smile.

Finally he said, "Look, thanks for helping me."

I thought perhaps he was referring to the night I went with him to Julie's apartment, but I didn't feel I had been much help, and the whole event seemed like a dream to me anyway. I decided instead that he was referring to the whole counseling encounter that we experienced together over the past two and a half years.

I said, "That's OK. I have learned a lot myself."

Then David said, "You know, over the last few months, I've done a lot of thinking. Before, my decisions about things were pretty shaky, but lately...well, I feel a bit more sane. And, well...I've made some decisions and I wanted to run them by you. I mean, since you're my shrink and all." He had a slight grin on his face as he made the shrink remark.

As I sat listening to David talk, I found myself now thinking about him differently than ever before. Rather than dreading him, I marveled at him. Rather than wanting to run for the hills, I actually anticipated him entering my office. What a turnaround!

I also thought, *I really didn't do that much to help David. He did most of the talking. I just listened. I really can't claim it was my great knowledge and wisdom that made a difference for David. I can't even say it was my huge love and compassion, because most of the time I wanted to avoid him altogether.*

David continued, "I've decided as much as I don't like to talk to people about what I'm feeling, I can't do that anymore. I'm not the kind of person who can afford to hold all my stuff in, so I'm going to talk to someone when I feel certain things. My partner isn't such a bad guy. Who knows? Maybe I'll start talking to him, although he might have a heart attack. I don't think I've said more than fifty words to him since they put us together. And you'll be proud of me. I actually did talk to Susan a little bit. I told her about how it hurt me when Steve was killed. And I thought she really did have a heart attack. She stared at me like she thought I flipped out. If she only knew. When she realized I was being honest, she started to cry and gave me a hug. It felt pretty good."

I wanted to shout for all I was worth, but David didn't give me a chance.

He went on, "I've also decided that I need to start keeping a list of organizations that help people in need, rather than me thinking I have to carry their problems all by myself. That is what I was doing with Julie. They give us phone numbers to call, but I never used them, because I wasn't sure how much they really cared. I should have given Julie a *phone number*, not a bunch of hamburgers. That way I can feel like I don't have to worry about people as much. If they want help, they can make the effort and get it for themselves."

"Anyway," he said, "that's what I've decided. What do you think?"

I was so surprised I was speechless. I didn't say anything

for several seconds, enough time it seemed to make David feel uncomfortable. Finally I said, "David, I think you have made some awesome choices. I'm really proud of you."

David went on telling me more about some of the things he thought about since our last meeting, and I was intrigued, but largely I was amazed.

At no place during our many sessions had I ever thought that David would turn out normal. I was convinced that he might improve somewhat and maybe increase the function ability factor in his life to a degree. But normal…I didn't think it was possible. He was too crazy, and the explosive potential within him was way too evident. Yet here he was, analyzing his own condition, perhaps more insightfully than I.

Two hours went by like a few moments.

That day I talked to David about beginning a relationship with God, which he did. I also invited him to come to church sometime. He was nice about the invitation, but I could tell he still felt as if his anonymity were something he needed to protect. I could see in his eyes he felt that attending our church even once might be the one mistake that would not only jeopardize his privacy, it may also end his career. So I recommended another church for him to attend.

I prayed with him at the end of our time that day and he left. As I watched him leave I wondered as I had a few times before if God sent David to me for a greater purpose than for just his healing. I wondered if it could be in God's plan that I wasn't David's teacher, but instead he was mine.

As I sat there that day pondering these things, I recalled a startling incident that took place somewhere around the time David first entered my life.

In addition to my pastoral leadership, I also supervised about eighteen churches in my denomination. One day I received a call from one of my superiors asking me to attend a meeting together with several leaders. It was an unusual time and occasion for a meeting, and I was concerned and unsettled as the day of the event approached.

When I arrived at the location on the designated day, I was ushered into a room with seventeen other men who held similar positions to mine. We sat in a circle of chairs that were prearranged to accommodate the whole group of us. There were four or five empty chairs with reserved signs on them that were in the circle as well. When we were all in place, three key leaders in our denomination and our district overseer marched into the room and took the seats that were reserved.

Our overseer was very dear to us. We trusted him and counted on him as our leader and friend. He supervised the eighteen of us as we oversaw the churches under our care. We were a team, a well-oiled and crisp operating team. We all respected and trusted each other implicitly, but we had a sense that our structure was about to be dismantled.

The person leading the meeting called our attention to himself. He then prayed, asking God for wisdom to speak with clarity and to be understood. He then informed us that our beloved supervisor, who kept his head pointed to the ground from the time he entered the room, committed an indiscretion. He was involved in an adulterous affair over a five-year period.

Upon hearing the announcement we all sat dumbfounded. We were in shock. Then, one-by-one, we began to weep. Soon all of us were crying uncontrollably. We wept and sobbed for what seemed to be an eternity. Perhaps twenty minutes later our crying subsided, but we were numb.

I personally felt pain—intense pain.

I felt pain for my supervisor whom I loved and respected with every ounce of my being.

I felt the pain of betrayal. I felt he let me down personally.

I felt the pain of loss. It wasn't the loss of relationship or friendship. It was the loss of trust. I gave my full trust to this man, but that day, and for some time, I didn't know to whom I could give my trust.

I resolved these things in time, but the announcement that day hit me so hard. I knew I would not be the same. Over time serious philosophical repercussions occurred in my thinking that would eventually change my approach to life and ministry forever. Oddly enough, I had an inkling of some of those changes that very day. I didn't know what would change. I only knew something would. I didn't form those adjustments in my mind then. I couldn't. There was no sound thinking available to me at that moment. But something told me my whole approach to ministry was about to be altered as a result of the events of that day.

Over time I analyzed many of the foundational premises I held regarding ministry, premises my supervisor held as well. I started to repel those that didn't seem sound and embrace those that did. I would have never questioned anything had I not been presented with the challenge to question him. Now I found myself reconsidering a myriad of ministry ideals.

He was one of the leaders in my life who praised me before others for having a growing church in my early ministries and spoke words of disapproval for those whose churches didn't grow. He embraced values that lent support to church growth and bigger parishes and was very inclined toward promotions and successes in the ministry. I was forced, after the day of that devastating announcement, to reevaluate all of his premises that mingled with mine, especially those that seemed inappropriate to me.

I remember thinking that my supervisor would never have understood the time I put in with David. He would have advised me to avoid him, let him down easy, or refer him to someone else. I suspected that he would have suggested that I put my time into my own people and insist on an appointment rather than drop-in sessions. I had a sense that if my supervisor knew about David, as soon as I discovered that this detective was not a potential to attend our church, he would have advised me to drop him as I would a nasty habit. I remember feeling that these would be the thoughts of my supervisor, and that is why I never told him about David. I can't say for sure that is the way he would have responded, but that was the impression I had.

Early on I actually had some of those same thoughts about David. If I acted on these thoughts, which I presumed were also in my supervisor's heart, I would have missed all God wanted to teach me through my association with David.

In spite of his mistake I still love and respect my former supervisor. I don't judge him flawed because of his ways of thinking about ministry. His heart may have been much more pure than mine.

No. It was my own thinking God wanted to unravel and cleanse. He used a strain of thoughts, similar to my own, in someone I loved and trusted to impress on me that I should consider reshaping that way of thinking in my own heart.

It didn't happen overnight. It took several years for me to examine my values with regard to church growth, bigger churches, and success in the ministry and reconstruct them into a framework I felt at peace with. It would never have happened if something hadn't occurred to shake my confidence in my own thinking processes.

I have found over the years that I am very capable of believing with my whole heart something that is entirely incorrect. And then, in order to fend off criticism concerning the issue, I will build a structural defense around that belief in order to ensure that it doesn't get dismantled by anyone. This way I can ward off feeling threatened and think I am right all at the same time. I spent thirty-five years building a belief structure in my own life that was strong but wrong. It would take a shocking event and much time to deconstruct it, and then even more time to reconstruct a correct belief structure to take its place.

I have also found this is one of the most unsettling aspects of ministry and our relationship with the Father. God loves us just as we are; flaws, blemishes, warts, and all. He will allow us to make all manner of mistakes on our journey toward the refined product He is producing. Just about the time we think we have the correct perspective on the way things should be, regarding kingdom matters and our relationship with Him, He will show us where we were all wrong.

I remember, in my early days of ministry, standing before my congregation and preaching things I believed with all my being. My entire life and ministry was founded upon some of the things I preached in those days. But now I wouldn't be caught dead saying those same things. I've changed my opinion about them completely. Any foundation made up of our human ideas is shaky. The only reason I didn't fall flat is because the foundation I built my ultimate spiritual existence upon was firm. It is the rock, Christ Jesus. Ideas, opinions, and ministry methods can change, and often need to, but He alone is our rock. I have learned I need to allow Him to alter and dismantle the structure in my life as He chooses. As long as the foundation stays the same, I will be fine.

God seems delighted to shake up the supporting beams of our lives in an effort to see fresh perspectives formed in our hearts; perspectives that are designed to cause our thinking to be more like His.

CHAPTER 14

Final Visit

David came back one more time about two months after his previous visit.

He slid into my office one day with a sheepish look on his face. We engaged in small talk for a few minutes, but all the while I could see he was laboring over something that was heavy on his mind.

Finally he asked a question as a conversation filler, "So, how is your church doing?"

What David didn't know was that on that particular day, neither my church nor I was doing very well at all. I was still reeling from the "earthquake exodus."

I don't know what got into me. I am usually careful to not dump my dirty laundry on people who I am trying to help and who have enough trouble taking care of their own issues. But David's question caught me off guard.

In response to his question I said, "You know what, David? Our church isn't doing very well at all." I went on to say, "And I'm not doing very well either."

He looked a little surprised. To him I always seemed to be so *together*. I don't think he really wanted to show interest in

what might be my struggles or even my successes. I rather
think he was nervous that day about what he came to tell
me. His question to me probably reflected the awkwardness
he felt. He didn't expect to get an earful.

To make things even more difficult for him, I wasn't at all
in touch with his needs that day, at least not to start with.
Instead I was overwhelmed with my own.

I jumped into a half-guarded, half-whining description
about how tired I was of working myself ragged to help
people, and just about the time the church seems to be
coming together, another setback occurs.

I alluded to the pain I felt over losing forty people to the
earthquake, but I wasn't really talking about the earthquake.
I wasn't even talking about the eight years I spent at that
church, trying and failing, growing and declining, being
encouraged and then being let down. I was talking about all
of the early experiences of nongrowth and little success in
my ministry. I was talking about my whole life.

Poor David! He did not come that day to hear all that.

I remember saying to him with an almost sassy cynicism,
"I know the earthquake was out of my control, but
I sometimes wonder if I have ever done anything for God.
I wonder if I have ever touched anyone in a way that has
really made a difference in that person's life." I said, "It seems
as if everyone I touch isn't helped enough by my ministry to
stay committed to it."

I don't know why I was so careless to say such things to
David. He did not become a confidant or a counselor. He
had some serious issues of his own, and it was extremely
unprofessional of me to unload on him.

To all of that David responded with a statement that would, over time, reshape my whole way of thinking about the ministry. He was not trying to be profound. I am certain to this day that he has no idea about the impact his next words had on me.

He said, "Well, I don't know about everyone else in your ministry, but you have touched this one," as he pointed his thumb at his chest, "and I'll never be the same."

He looked at me when he said it, but then he looked away as if he left himself way too vulnerable by giving me that tender of a compliment. It was extremely uncharacteristic of anything I saw from David in all the sessions I had with him. He seemed almost uncaring, so totally absorbed with his own pain that he was incapable of encouraging someone else.

At that, tears came to my eyes, and I was brought back to reality.

I said, "David, thank you for saying that." I went on, "I'm sorry for unloading all of my garbage onto you. You just caught me in a bad way on a bad day."

We put the previous conversational issues to rest, and I said, "David, you didn't come to counsel me today. How are you doing? What can I do for you?"

The sheepish look he entered my office with that day returned to his face, and he said, "Well…uh…this is probably my last visit."

I said, "Really?" with genuine surprise.

He said, "Yeah. I'm going to be moving."

"Moving where?" I asked, hoping my displeasure didn't show. I was feeling at that point that displaying disappointment over his leaving would have been almost pathological on my part considering the big deal I made earlier about people leaving my church. So I tried to temper my disappointment.

In response to my question he answered, "Well, that's the miracle. I'm going to be moving to a state in the Midwest. I have been asked to become the police chief in a small town there, and I said yes."

A deluge of questions came to my mind, but all of them seemed inappropriate to ask, so I refrained. Instead I rejoiced with him.

"That's great, David. Congratulations! How soon will you be leaving?"

"This week," he said. "I know I should have told you sooner, but I have been pretty busy getting all of my stuff together; you know, the paperwork, my house, and my family. I knew I needed to get by here before I left so I could tell you."

"That's OK. I understand," I said consolingly.

"Listen," he said while looking at the floor, "I want to thank you for all you did to help me. I know it wasn't easy for you to listen to all my junk." Then he looked up, but not directly at me, and said, "Especially when I would just pop in and take so much of your time. I don't know what I would have done if you hadn't listened to me. You know, I went by four other churches before I came here, and they all chased me away. You were my last hope. If you turned me away, I already determined I wasn't going back to another minister."

Then he paused, and I thought I saw his eyes well up. He looked straight at me and said, "Thank you. Thank you for saving my life."

With that he reached over to shake my hand and said, "I have to go. Maybe we will see each other again someday."

Then David turned and walked out my door. I watched him walk to his car, get in, and drive off. As he did, I was filled with emotions.

I know I felt a sense of joy, because God gave me the opportunity to genuinely help someone who was in a very bad way.

I also felt a bit foolish for my unprofessional behavior.

I felt sadness. I was going to miss David. He wasn't a buddy, but there was a clear sense of satisfaction that I started to feel in my times with him, and I would surely miss that.

I also felt somewhat uneasy for the people in that midwestern town, because I wasn't sure whether or not David was really healed. The third word on the scratch sheet I placed in my counseling file was *upbringing*. I never had the opportunity to talk with David about this third subject, and I felt as if there were probably some issues from his childhood that played out in David's behavior. The presence of mind to bring this up to David didn't reveal itself until he was well out the driveway. I wasn't sure I would have felt the freedom to confront him about it anyway.

More than anything, I felt a sense of loss. I felt as if a person came into my life, captured my heart, and left me to deal with the pain of having to forfeit that relationship. To make it more difficult, there was no consolation in the hope that I could call him and reminisce about old times, or check up on him to make sure he was doing all right. I didn't have a clue as to where he was going. It seemed clear his better judgment determined it was best for him that I didn't know.

I took a deep breath and started to think on what he said to me.

Was *touching one person* what the ministry was all about? Obviously I don't mean touching only one person for my whole ministry. I knew that wasn't at all true in my life. I was privileged to touch many in the course of my ministry up to that point, but was *touching one person at a time* a valid ministry objective? Was the highly focused attention I was compelled to give to David when he arrived on my doorstep what Jesus wanted from me more than my ministry to quantities of people? It would certainly make sense biblically, considering the individual and focused concern His Word suggests God has for each of us.

I witnessed a transformation in David's life over the months and years I spent with him. I remember thinking that the fulfillment I felt because of that transformation was high on the satisfaction charts for me. I didn't feel at the time that David would be pivotal in helping me to reshape all of my thinking about church growth. I certainly didn't know I would write a book with David as the central character. And yet I had a sense that the whole counseling scenario with David was a uniquely planned experience provided for my growth by the Lord.

CHAPTER 15

An Old Value

I thought the time I spent with Detective David was extensive until I added it up. After I totaled all the hours I spent with him over a two to three year period, it only came to about thirty-five hours...total. Granted, most of them were surprise hours, time I wasn't prepared to sacrifice, but they turned out to be some of the most well-spent hours of my ministry. Those visits would ultimately be responsible for forming within me a core value concerning ministry that has shaped me for eternity.

Jesus was followed by the masses. Wherever He went, crowds thronged Him. At times, He tried to retreat from the people only to have them chase after Him, because they desired more of Him. Yet it was His ministry style, even when He was intent on another objective, to stop and give His full attention to some needy individual who interrupted His progress toward His goal.

He stopped to *touch one*, to focus on *one*, to meet the need of *one*.

The ministry is *touching one* over and over again.

Some people are very needy. They have emotional issues

that require great amounts of attention; attention that most people aren't equipped to deal with. Nor can most afford to give the literal *hundreds of hours* necessary to bring these people to a place of wholeness. So I am not talking about giving countless hours to extreme emotional cases.

I am not talking about becoming the intimate friend of every person in our sphere of influence. That would also be a mess. No one person, pastor, or otherwise has the emotional or practical ability to have a multitude of close relationships.

Nor am I talking about dumping huge amounts of time into high-maintenance individuals. Most are aware that there are certain people who require a great deal of maintenance while they achieve little or no growth. At the same time these people make an incredibly low impact in other people's lives, their own, or Christ's church. Putting much time into these kinds of people can turn one's life into an endless cycle of wheel spinning while making very little progress.

It seems to me, however, that God desires His servants to have a heart for *the one* as opposed to having a desire to reach *the masses*. There is a great amount of progress that can be made for Christ's kingdom by anyone willing to embrace this old but timeless value.

Each time David came to my office I wasn't prepared for him. Yet I felt compelled to minister to him. I can't explain what went through my mind. I just did not feel the liberty from God's Spirit to turn him away. I think the reason for this was that God wanted to teach me an important lesson. That lesson was, "*the one* matters to Him; and if *the one* matters to Him, *the one* should matter to me." If I minister *to one* with a need, I have done a huge work for God, even though my aspirations for success may not have been realized.

I also feel that God wanted to say to me through David's visits, "If you are too busy to help *one* person (like David) then you are way too busy. If you are too busy to *touch the one* you may meet along the way—the *one* who may come as an interruption to your objectives and your schedule—then you have ceased to follow in the footsteps of Jesus." With Jesus, *the one* in need always took precedence over any objective He pursued, whether it was a location, an appointment, or a ministry.

"Think big," they tell us today. In today's vernacular, thinking big has the ring of *great exploits* and *growing larger* with *lofty* achievements. However, thinking big may be small thinking in God's economy. On the flip side, thinking small may be big thinking in God's economy.

I have decided that I will have done a big work for God when I have genuinely helped someone. If I begin to think about the potential increase to the size of my church or the respect or acclaim it might bring me then I am beginning to think small. God sees our need for acclaim to be a carnal and sinful desire. Just because I seek those things through the means of His kingdom ministry doesn't make them any more holy. If we seek a bigger ministry or a larger spiritual influence so we will feel better about our carnal selves, it's my feeling that God would delight, for the sake of His holiness, to knock our ministries and our egos down to size.

A THEOLOGY OF ONE

The Bible speaks very convincingly about the *theology of one*. Even the idea of fewer is often emphasized in favor of more, and less is frequently what God shoots for to accomplish His purposes.

In Luke 15 the shepherd leaves the ninety-nine sheep to focus his attention on *the one* who is lost. Then the woman puts all aside in her schedule, as well as her other nine coins, to search for *the one* lost coin, because it holds great worth to her. The point of both of these parables is to show the heavenly Father's heart for *the one* who is lost and in need.

Jesus was constantly followed by *the masses*, but He gave His time to *twelve*, His greater attention to *three* (Peter, James, and John), and His focused love *to one* (John).

When His discernment revealed wrongly motivated hearts in the throngs of people following Him (John 6), Jesus purposely discouraged them and watched them all desert Him. Then He gave *the twelve* the option to back out as well, suggesting He was willing to start over again with *just one*, Himself, if need be.

In the first chapter of the Bible, God used *one* man, Adam, to begin a race.

In Genesis 6 God used *one* man, Noah, to preserve that race.

In Genesis 12 God used *one* man, Abraham, to begin a nation.

In Exodus He used *one* man, Moses, to deliver that nation. Then in the face of this nation's failure in the wilderness, God made it clear He was quite willing to eliminate the whole lot of them and start over with Moses alone.

In the Book of Joshua God used *one* man by the same name to lead a nation into conquest.

In Judges He used *one* man, Gideon, to rescue *one* of Israel's twelve tribes. Then through him, God whittled an army of thirty-two thousand down to less than 1 percent of that to show Gideon and His people that God doesn't need the power of many.

In 1 Kings God used *one* man, Elijah, to rid the nation Israel of the influence of false prophets.

In Ezra God used *one* man to reestablish temple worship in Jerusalem after seventy years of exile. At the same time, He used *one* man, Nehemiah, to lead a reconstruction effort on the broken down walls of that great city.

In Esther God used *one* woman to save His nation from annihilation.

The criteria He used to choose these individuals was not great influence, great ability, or proven success. It was simple faith, trust, and passion for God. He looked at their humble hearts and determined they possessed the "right stuff" to minister for Him. God has never focused on *the multitudes*. He has always focused on *the one*. To accomplish His plans God doesn't need many who may represent earthly power. He only needs *one*, or at least fewer, with the right hearts.

Consider with me Elizabeth, the mother of John the Baptist. Do we think less of her because she is not known for ministering to quantities of people? She had *one* important task to perform in God's scheme to save the world. She needed to do the best job she could as she and her husband Zacharias reared *the one* who would go before and prepare the way for the Messiah.

Consider with me Mary, the mother of Jesus. What an extraordinary woman she was indeed! Yet we remember her primarily because of her ministry to *one* single individual. Do we consider her to be less significant because she wasn't focused on ministering to the masses? Of course not!

The same is true of Simeon and Anna the prophetess. Barnabas is best known for his ministry to *one* man, Paul, who was almost solely responsible for launching the whole concept of world missions.

Ephesians 4:4–6 tells us, "There is *one* body and *one* Spirit…*one* hope…*one* Lord, *one* faith, *one* baptism; *one* God and Father of all" (emphasis added).

Matthew 10:20 informs us that this *one* God numbers the hairs on each *one* of our heads.

Zephaniah 3:17 says that He joys over each *one* of us with singing.

Jeremiah 31:34 tells us that He remembers the sins of each *one* of us no more.

Psalms 56:8 tenderly reminds us that He puts the tears of each *one* of us in a bottle.

Psalms 139 says that He is aware of the following details of each *one* of our lives:

- He searches each *one* of us to know us thoroughly.

- He knows when each *one* of us sits down and stands up.

- He knows the thoughts of each *one* of us.

- He knows each *one* of our paths, when and where each *one* of us lies.

- He is acquainted with every way each *one* of us takes.

We cannot forget the parable of the good Samaritan in Luke 10 where a person of the despised ethnicity, the Samaritans, is *the one* who is the hero of the story. As Jesus tells it, this Samaritan is *the one* whom Jesus approves as having the proper compassion for the hurting individual on the side of the road, as opposed to the two "holy men" who didn't. The Samaritan stops his journey to help *one* troubled soul. He bandages the man's wounds, takes him to an inn, cares for him overnight, and pays for his stay for several days. He then offers more support to ensure that the man's recovery is provided for. Then Jesus leaves no uncertainty as to who has done the right thing—*the one* who stopped for *the one*. He tells all of us to "go and do likewise" (v. 37).

What is wrong with *touching one* person? Why do we feel we have to *touch the masses*? Why do we feel we have to minister to large quantities of people? Is it an ego thing with some of us? Are we slaves to the consumer mind-set of our age that shouts to us that *big, more,* and *many* are better than *small, less,* and *few*? In God's economy this is not true at all.

I had a professor in Bible college who would teach his standard lessons most days. His name was Mr. Starr. Some days, however, he would finish early, close his notebook, and talk to us about different things that tugged at his heartstrings, hoping something he might say would make a difference in some young student's life.

Sometimes he would say, "You know that Jesus' mission was to save the whole world, don't you?" When he received a nod he would continue, "And you know, each person you meet is a little world; a world in himself…a world, in herself. If you minister to just *one* person your whole life, you have ministered to a whole world; a small world, yes, but a whole world nonetheless."

When Brother Starr would say this, I would yawn and consider the minutes he devoted to his little discourse as down time until the end of class. You see, this kind of thinking had no real meaning for me. I was going to be a "teach the masses" kind of guy. Numbers and ever-increasing quantities of people were what I was going to be about. Ministering to *one* person at a time was small thinking. I guess he shared this one heart issue enough so that at the very least it got into my memory, if not my heart.

Now I understand why he talked about it.

He wanted to go against the grain of our consumer-focused culture. He wanted to help each of us ambitious young college students see that while our ministry was to the whole world, if we would simply consider each person we connect with as an entire world in him or herself, then we would give each *one* we touch the love and attention they deserved and needed. If we would do that we would be treating them as Jesus would treat them and we would be doing our part to reach the whole world.

Brother Starr also tried to bring ministry into perspective for us. He tried to help us bite off a portion we could easily chew. The ministry doesn't have to be complicated or overwhelming. There are hosts of people who are so overcome by the great accomplishments of some in the ministry that they consider themselves unqualified to even so much as *touch one*. Their little contribution is best not offered, because it looks shameful in the face of so many superior exploits. This wise professor simply challenged the myth that *many* and *more* are better than *less* and *few*. He said, "Don't miss the great work of ministering to *the one* that God has commissioned you to because you have listened to the lie that the only ministry that matters is a ministry to *many*."

Old Brother Starr also knew that most people don't make the effort to minister to even *one*, because most are shy or feel inhibited or inadequate or stressed and overcome by life. But if he could get us to care about each *one* we meet, as if that *one* person were the whole world, we would probably do more than most people do in a lifetime, even if that *one* person is the only person we ever touch.

It was great wisdom. I only wish I would have had the foresight to catch old Brother Starr's heart much earlier in my ministry.

The growth of the church of Jesus Christ over the last two thousand years cannot be attributed to mass presentations and responses to the gospel. The first evangelical sermon preached by Peter on the Day of Pentecost netted three thousand souls. But since then evangelism has been a *one-on-one* phenomenon—*one* person sharing Christ with another person, *one* at a time. Many may be able to cite mass conversions at rallies or crusades they have attended. If the details of every conversion were known, usually there would be a *one-on-one* example or testimony or witnessing going on before the event took place with each *one* who bowed the knee to Christ.

Billy Graham has seen millions respond to his sermons at crusades, but examining his evangelistic methods reveals the true source of his great numbers. He encouraged Christians in the area where he was going to minister months before his crusades, to build relationships with individuals. Then when he came to town, they were to bring those individuals with them to his meetings. This would help to ensure that trust before and relational follow-up afterward would be built into the process.

When you think about it, doesn't it stand to reason that the gospel would be spread worldwide *one* at a time? Jesus didn't commission us to share His gospel to the world by way of mass proclamation. He commissioned us in Acts 1 to be witnesses of Him. Being a witness requires closeness. It requires *one-on-one* contact. Regardless of where we go— Jerusalem, Judea, Samaria, or unto the uttermost parts of the earth—our witness for the Savior will only be effective if we get close to people *one* at a time.

The real power of evangelism is *one-on-one*.

These days I don't think much about reaching the masses. I am not opposed to God doing more through me, but I don't wallow in self-pity and beat myself up for being inadequate, because He doesn't. And I don't chase those illusive *thirty-eight seconds of glory* anymore. I've learned of the unworthiness of that objective. It is like sparkling diamonds to the eyes but broken glass to the touch. It shines like gold as we pursue it, but it crumbles like ashes when we grasp it.

Instead I think more about *the one*. I think about the one

worker open to spiritual things that God brings by my house to repair our sink. I think about *the one* stranded motorist I see on the side of the highway. I think about *the one* single parent needing to see Christ's love through me. I think about *the one* person I may encounter whom God sends across my path at the mall or the grocery store. I don't think about how that person might help to accomplish my success aspirations or add to my church's attendance or weekly offering totals. I simply try to think about how I can help that *one* person to see Jesus in me, so I can introduce him or her to the Savior.

David taught me to love and care about people for *who they are* and for what the Lord can do for them through me…not for how my ministry and I can benefit from them.

Have I seen the ministries I lead grow since my "David 101" experience? Yes. But I am much more excited about the growth that has taken place in me—that being the worth I feel whether my ministry grows or not. And I feel it largely because I have discovered—and have begun to embrace— God's heart for the one.

CHAPTER 16

The Potential of One

We have all heard of the stories of people who have been examples to just *one* person. Yet that *one* person grew up to be a great and influential evangelist, church leader, or missionary.

I am not a Billy Graham or the leader of a huge church, but when I was growing up, there was *one* young man who made a profound impression on me. He taught my teenage Sunday school class. He never wrote a book or went into the ministry full-time. He didn't pastor a church or lead a revival, but he was always there. His name was John Porter, and John Porter *touched this one life*.

At no time did he know what I would become; preacher, politician, or transient. In fact I was quite the rascal. I'm sure he had plenty of doubts about me, but he kept on loving me.

I am also sure John had no aspirations about having the largest teenage boys' Sunday school class in the town of Westfield, New York, where I grew up. Nor did John think if he *touched this one life* named Chris, maybe I would become great and that would bring greatness his way. He just loved

kids and loved *touching them with his one life one at a time.*
As he did, he got into my heart. He didn't even know how
he impacted me and probably doesn't to this day. But he
did, and I thank him for it, and I thank God for him. John
brought credence to the term "There is incredible potential
in *one.*"

In the early nineties a stirring film hit the theatres.
Schindler's List grabbed the hearts of people all over the world.
It created much controversy, some of which surrounded the
artistry of the movie. It was shown in black and white, but
at one point in the story, Oscar Schindler began to see color.
He started to see the masses of Jewish people who were
being slaughtered by the Nazi's as individuals, and it was
illustrated by a touch of red.

We were moved when out of the muddy gray effect of
black and white cinematography, *one* lone little girl stood
out in a red dress. With his eyes from an upstairs window,
Schindler followed this lone child dressed in crimson as
she walked down a war-torn avenue. As his eyes were
affixed to her trek down the gray tinted street, at times she
would disappear behind an obstacle or a group of people.
Her brief disappearances caused Schindler to mildly panic
and desperately search the street with his eyes in an effort
to relocate her body draped in red. This visual effect was
intended to demonstrate that Schindler crossed a line. He
could no longer view the Jews as a mass of people deserving
annihilation. He must now consider them to be individuals;
single, valuable, mistreated individuals.

He noticed *the one,* and it grabbed him down deep in his
soul. At that moment he began to care. He began to see the

Jewish people as people of true worth even though they were being extricated in large quantities and were of zero value to the Nazi Regime.

When Schindler lost momentary sight of this girl, his desperation to find her reflected something else. It reflected a virtuousness and righteousness that he allowed to be loosed in his soul. What he was starting to feel about this little girl felt good. He wasn't sure where it came from, but it seemed wholesome, and it made him feel clean. It felt like the joy and peace God wants us to experience when we think and feel rightly. Oscar Schindler took a vital step, crossing over into Godlike compassion, and it changed his life.

God feels this same compassion for *the one* at all times, but more than for just *one* little girl dressed in red. He feels it about all of us and sees each of us as individuals at the same time, similar to the way Oscar Schindler saw this *one* lone girl. Why does God see us that way? Because He is holy and righteous, and His mercy extends to all generations.

Not only does God see us with compassionate eyes, He sees us with eyes that perceive our potential. When His sight falls upon us (which is always), He sees all things of worth about us.

I can recall standing before large crowds of people at various times early in my ministry. Sadly I don't remember ever noticing individuals in the crowd. I didn't single out people and try to sense a person's need, feel someone's pain, or detect a lonely heart. Instead, when the gathering was over, I thought about how I looked and what people felt about me and what I said. Now, however, I find myself becoming more aware of the individuals before me rather than the crowds before me. I see their needs and fears, their hopes and dreams. I hope it is because I am becoming more like my heavenly Father. I think it is.

Have you ever lumped people into a group and labeled them?

"This kind of person is lazy."

"Those who react as he does are rebellious."

"Any with her kind of attitude are impossible to work with."

Usually we write these people off as incorrigible and determine not to bother with them. I've done this. In fact I have used this method of discernment concerning the attitudes of people quite successfully and have prided myself in avoiding some train wrecks in the ministry as a result.

Take note of an unfortunate outcome of this way of thinking.

I have written people off more than once and was not at all grieved when they migrated away from me and eventually left my church, probably because they felt alienation from me. Then to my surprise, a year or two or five later, I ran into them again. Also to my surprise they changed. They became broken, humble, or completely altered by God's transforming power.

My first thought was positive. I felt thankful that God performed a good work in their lives. My second thought, however, was more self-condemning.

I gave up on that person, but God had not. As Oscar Schindler, He kept His eye on them, not letting them out of His sight. Even more so, God kept His eye on the potential gifts, talents, and worth He knew was within them. Their potential stood out to Him as a bright red set of clothes in a dull gray environment. Consequently He never considered them *throw-away* as I had.

Worse yet, God allowed that person to hook up with another Christian, pastor, or church leader who was better than I—one who was able to see the potential in that person when I was not; one who was able to love and nurture that individual to become the person God always knew he or she could become.

As well, when I saw these people humble and transformed, I recognized a distinct hollow feeling in the pit of my stomach. I didn't feel it because I lost them to another church, but because I missed their potential. Perhaps I was too focused on my ministry, my success, my future, and ultimately myself. Maybe I was just out of *touch*. Regardless, the Lord sifted me, because I was someone who was unable to see in them what God always saw. God had to bring them to someone, who, like Himself, cared enough about them to be able to see their potential. This thought hit me like a punch in the gut.

When God sees us, He also sees everything good about us. He sees our possibilities, talents, gifts, abilities, hopes, dreams, futures, and incredible potentials. Why does He see these things? He sees them, because He is love.

We, on the other hand, tend to see people's faults, failures, shortcomings, mistakes, inconsistencies, and lack of potential, because we are less like love and more like indifference. Love sees the good in people. Indifference sees the negative…or nothing.

I'm told that a trip to Calcutta and a tour of the poorest

parts of the city will reveal a great deal of despair and hopelessness. Young children sit on the street corners and amid cardboard shanties. They sit with sores, disease, and obvious defects on their bodies. They sit almost motionless and without expression, waiting for someone to give them a morsel of food. They don't look at you with hope, because they have none. Instead, they peer at you with hollow, blank eyes. When you give them something, they don't show enthusiasm, because they don't have the emotional energy to offer such an emotion. When you give them nothing, they don't respond with disappointment, because they did not looked at you with anticipation in the first place. Instead they just look away emotionless and stare straight ahead as if the concept of hope was an unfamiliar value to them. No one considers them to be diamonds in the rough, potential leaders, or possible future men and women of promise.

But God does. He knows that within their hearts they have lost hope somewhere along the way and that they gave up at a very early age. Although they themselves and the people who pass them by each day see no potential in them, God has a keen read on their great worth.

If you will think on that for even a short while, it will change your opinion about God forever. God sees worth even in those we, and the entire world, consider worthless.

When David first came to me and while early sessions were passing by, I saw little hope for him and virtually no worth in him. I saw a man dripping with lunacy and headed for a lifetime sentence of craziness with no chance for a reprieve. I wanted to get rid of him any way I could and was sure every minute I spent with him was a complete waste of time.

God knew better. He knew David had great worth, and He wanted me to discover it too. I guess God even saw worth in me.

Earlier in this chapter I said my Sunday school teacher, John Porter, influenced me for Christ. He didn't know what I would become. He merely cared. Lest I communicate that I believe God saw potential in me and positioned John to be an influencer in my life, what I really want to say is this: The potential God observed had little to do with me. It had all to do with John Porter.

We are so prone to give the Billy Grahams and the Billy Sundays of this world credit for having the most potential, because they have the great names, have reached the huge numbers, and have held the massive crusades. But the Johns, Joes, Sams, and Jims of this world who influence the great and the not-so-great names, are the ones we have to stop and acknowledge. Why? Because God considers them worth as much as those with lofty names and accomplishments. It was their lives that possessed the hidden talent, personality, and influence that impressed the Billys and similar evangelists and Christian leaders to consider Christ. It was their lives that truly cared. It was their lives that were holy and genuine, loving and Godlike. It was their lives that God positioned to intersect with those who would otherwise not come to the Lord through any other witness.

I liken it to a great river. The mighty Colorado is an excellent example. If you were to climb upstream to the headwaters of the Colorado River, you would find its source to be about twenty-five miles north of Granby, Colorado, positioned between two twelve-thousand-foot-high mountain peaks in Rocky Mountain National Park, and just a few hundred feet west of the Continental Divide. At its headwaters the river is less than three feet wide. A child could easily jump across the Colorado at its source.

Many would say the causes of the great river's size are numerous, and those causes have names. They are the names of literally hundreds of streams that empty into the Colorado along its journey to the Pacific Ocean by way of the Gulf of California. As they meet up with the river, its size increases and the volume of water it carries multiplies exponentially as it moves along.

I'd like to offer another perspective. I would suggest that the true origin of the Colorado's great size is the positioning of its source. If the headwaters of the mighty Colorado were not situated exactly where they are, the river would not snake through the many Colorado canyons the way it does. Because of the path it takes, which starts high in the Rockies, the river is able to collect the offerings of the many rivers that flow into it. As a result the Colorado eventually becomes a huge river of influence providing vital fresh water for Colorado, Arizona, Utah, Nevada, and the millions of people in California.

I believe the same is true of the many great men and women of faith today. The true cause of the good God does through them is the positioning of their source. It starts with God, of course. But next it is the person or persons God planted into their lives who guided them to Christ. It's those who were their early mentors. It's their first Christian influencer, their first genuine witness who impacted them to get started right. It is someone who cared about *the one.*

They are great, because they *touched the one*. It's probable that they saw no halos over the people they ministered to and had no visions about their soon-to-be converts. It's likely that they had no prophecies or premonitions about the people they were leading to the foot of the cross. They were merely caring for the one God placed in their path, and that is the miracle of their lives. They just cared.

I was recently introduced to a business model, the structure of which is ingeniously designed to unearth pieces of coal (humanly speaking) and turn them into diamonds. *Potential* is their battle cry. They look for the type of people who have squandered early opportunities and whom society has now set aside—a stocker in a grocery store, a waiter in a restaurant, a college graduate who couldn't land a job in his or her field, or a clerk fired numerous times. Our culture has set them aside, because they work low-paying jobs or because they made early mistakes. This business model that has Christian leanings searches them out and turns them into the great people God intended them to be, financially and independently free. And they, in turn, look for other *diamonds in the rough* and do the same with them. I bought into the business just because I wanted to be exposed to and nurtured by its wholesome and positive environment. It is an awesome system, but it's not one that is fully understood by our culture today.

Here's my point! There is potential for greatness in every person, regardless of social class, education, race, upbringing, or reputation. Can you see it? Are you able to peer through the outward appearances and see past your own preconceived notions about why people are the way they are? Are you able to see what God sees?

A human being of worth...

A person of value...

A life uniquely and divinely designed by the Creator, fashioned for greatness...

Here's a test. Can you see worth in that little girl dressed in red? Can you see potential in her? She simply walked down a street, and she captured the attention of a man who would ultimately be responsible for saving a thousand people from the Nazi gas chambers. Forget the human arguments that explain away her value because she had no knowledge she was being watched. Can you see worth in her just because of the way God used her?

If you can see these kinds of things, you won't be swayed by the carnal values of man any longer. You won't allow yourself to be lied to by the opinions of people. *The one* will matter to you more than *the masses*. The achievement and welfare of others will matter more to you than your own success and accomplishments. Helping the underdog will find a greater place in your soul than having association with the wealthy and mighty.

CHAPTER 17

Dream On

O ne night I had a dream. I dreamed that I moved from California to Colorado and was preaching in a new church on my first Sunday. As the dream went, though in my conscious and awake mind I knew I was going to be restarting a church having no people, in my dream and on that first Sunday, every seat in the church was filled. And though, in my conscious mind, I knew what the church looked like from an earlier visit, the church in my dream was much larger in size and different in appearance.

The church building in my dream was rectangular in shape with the platform at one end and the entrance door at the other. The back wall of the church had large stained glass windows on either side of the entrance door and smaller windows lined each of the two sidewalls. The sun shone through the rear windows, creating an enormous glare. The entrance was a double-door and made of solid wood, allowing no light from the sun to enter as long as the door was closed.

In my dream I preached from the front center of the church on the platform. As I preached, the rear entrance door opened. When it did, it revealed an enormous, blinding, yellowish glare from the sun as the person who opened the door entered. I could not tell who that person was. The glare was too blinding. As I stood there preaching and watching this person come in, I had a sense and a hope that it was David.

Before the door eased to a closed position, this person, apparently a man, slipped into the back pew to his right and my left. He was wearing a hat. It was the kind of hat you would see a city detective wearing in a movie about gangsters set in the 1930s, and he wore a pin-striped double-breasted suit set in the same era. He nudged his way by the many people sitting in that row until he arrived at an empty seat in the middle. He never took off his hat. I was still unable to see him clearly, because the glare from the window behind him hindered my view.

He sat down, and I continued to preach my sermon. All the while, however, I kept looking in his direction in an effort to identify this man. But the glare from the sun shining through the window behind him refused to subside in intensity throughout my entire sermon. The mystery of his identity continued.

When I finally finished my sermon, I closed the service and dismissed the congregation. But my heart was intent on only one thing. I seemed desperate to get to the back of the church to greet this man whom I sensed and hoped was David. I moved into the center aisle and started toward the rear of the church.

But when dismissed, the people flooded into the aisles and blocked the way, making it difficult for me to get to the back.

I continued to press through the crowd with my eyes intent on this man, who also raised himself to a standing position with the rest of the people when I dismissed them. The glare from the sun, however, was just as strong as it was during the service so that I was still unable to discover exactly who the man was.

I began to feel frustration as I attempted to make my way to the back. But the harder I pushed, the thicker the crowd became, and the more difficult it was for me to make progress toward the rear. The people in the crowd weren't really interested in talking to me or getting up close to me. There were just too many of them, but I kept pressing down the center aisle, through the ever-burgeoning crowd and kept watching the man in the back.

As I watched and pressed through the crowd, the man with the detective hat moved through the back row and toward the center aisle as well. He didn't appear to be in a hurry, but I could see he was intent on the back door. The sun still shone brightly through the windows and the door that was now propped open. All I could see of the man was his outline as he reached the rear doors, exited, and headed for the parking lot. But the crowd in the center aisle kept holding me back. I had little concern about meeting the people who were in attendance on my first Sunday. I only wanted to reach this mysterious man.

Finally, after much anguish, I reached the rear doors of the church and ran outside and down the steps. Frantically I looked around and finally spotted the man. He was still wearing the detective hat, but he was in his car, which was by then pulling out of the parking lot. For some reason

I didn't run after him...I just knew. I knew it was David, but I also knew I wouldn't, nor was I supposed to, see him again. I just stood there by the steps I had just descended and watched as he pulled out of the lot, drove down the street, and disappeared.

With that, I awoke.